The Pentagon Papers

National Security Versus the Public's Right to Know

by Geoffrey A. Cambpell

FAMOUS

TRIALS

Lucent Books, San Diego, CA

Titles in the Famous Trials series include:

The Boston Massacre
Brown v. Board of Education
Cherokee Nation v. Georgia
The Dred Scott Decision
The Impeachment of Bill
Clinton
Miranda v. Arizona
The Nuremberg Trials
The O.J. Simpson Trial

Roe v. Wade
The Rosenberg Espionage
Case
The Salem Witch Trials
The Scopes Trial
The Trial of Adolf Eichmann
The Trial of Joan of Arc
The Trial of John Brown
The Trial of Socrates

Library of Congress Cataloging-in-Publication Data

Campbell, Geoffrey A.
    The Pentagon Papers : national security versus the public's right to know / by Geoffrey A. Campbell.
    p. cm. — (Famous trials)
    Includes bibliographical references and index.
    Summary: Discusses the Supreme Court trial which resulted from the decision of the *New York Times* newspaper to publish secret government documents about the Vietnam War.
    ISBN 1-56006-692-X (lib. : alk. paper)
    1. New York Times Company—Trials, litigation, etc.—Juvenile literature. 2. Pentagon Papers—Juvenile literature. 3. Security classification (Government documents)—United States—Juvenile literature. 4. Freedom of the Press—United States—Juvenile literature. 5. Vietnamese Conflict, 1961–1975—United States— Juvenile literature. [1. New York Times Company—Trials, litigation, etc. 2. Pentagon Papers. 3. Freedom of Speech. 4. Vietnamese Conflict, 1961–1975—United States.] I. Title. II. Series.
    KF228.N52 C36   2000
    342.73'0853—dc21   00-008083
                                                          CIP

Table of Contents

Foreword

"The law is not an end in and of itself, nor does it provide ends. It is preeminently a means to serve what we think is right."

William J. Brennan Jr.

THE CONCEPT OF JUSTICE AND THE RULE OF LAW are hallmarks of Western civilization, manifested perhaps most visibly in widely famous and dramatic court trials. These trials include such important and memorable personages as the ancient Greek philosopher Socrates, who was accused and convicted of corrupting the minds of his society's youth in 399 B.C.; the French maiden and military leader Joan of Arc, accused and convicted of heresy against the church in 1431; to former football star O.J. Simpson, acquitted of double murder in 1995. These and other well-known and controversial trials constitute the most public, and therefore most familiar, demonstrations of a Western legal tradition that dates back through the ages. Although no one is certain when the first law code appeared or when the first formal court trials were held, Babylonian ruler Hammurabi introduced the first known law code in about 1760 B.C. It remains unclear how this code was administered, and no records of specific trials have survived. What is clear, however, is that humans have always sought to govern behavior and define actions in terms of law.

Almost all societies have made laws and prosecuted people for going against those laws, but the question of which behaviors to sanction and which to censure has always been controversial and remains in flux. Some, such as Roman orator and legislator Cicero, argue that laws are simply applications of universal standards. Cicero believed that humanity would agree on what constituted illegal behavior and that human laws were a mere extension of natural laws. "True law is right reason in agreement with nature," he wrote,

4

world-wide in scope, unchanging, everlasting. . . . We may not oppose or alter that law, we cannot abolish it, we cannot be freed from its obligations by any legislature. . . . This [natural] law does not differ for Rome and for Athens, for the present and for the future. . . . It is and will be valid for all nations and all times.

Cicero's rather optimistic view has been contradicted throughout history, however. For every law made to preserve harmony and set universal standards of behavior, another has been born of fear, prejudice, greed, desire for power, and a host of other motives. History is replete with individuals defying and fighting to change such laws—and even to topple governments that dictate such laws. Abolitionists fought against slavery, civil rights leaders fought for equal rights, millions throughout the world have fought for independence—these constitute a minimum of reasons for which people have sought to overturn laws that they believed to be wrong or unjust. In opposition to Cicero, then, many others, such as eighteenth-century English poet and philosopher William Godwin, believe humans must be constantly vigilant against bad laws. As Godwin said in 1793:

Laws we sometimes call the wisdom of our ancestors. But this is a strange imposition. It was as frequently the dictate of their passion, of timidity, jealousy, a monopolizing spirit, and a lust of power that knew no bounds. Are we not obliged perpetually to renew and remodel this misnamed wisdom of our ancestors? To correct it by a detection of their ignorance, and a censure of their intolerance?

Lucent Books' *Famous Trials* series showcases trials that exemplify both society's praiseworthy condemnation of universally unacceptable behavior, and its misguided persecution of individuals based on fear and ignorance, as well as trials that leave open the question of whether justice has been done. Each volume begins by setting the scene and providing a historical context to show how society's mores influence the trial process and the verdict.

Each book goes on to present a detailed and lively account of the trial, including liberal use of primary source material such as direct testimony, lawyers' summations, and contemporary and modern commentary. In addition, sidebars throughout the text create a broader context by presenting illuminating details about important points of law, information on key personalities, and important distinctions related to civil, federal, and criminal procedures. Thus, all of the primary and secondary source material included in both the text and the sidebars demonstrates to readers the sources and methods historians use to derive information and conclusions about such events.

Lastly, each *Famous Trials* volume includes one or more of the following comprehensive tools that motivate readers to pursue further reading and research. A timeline allows readers to see the scope of the trial at a glance, annotated bibliographies provide both sources for further research and a thorough list of works consulted, a glossary helps students with unfamiliar words and concepts, and a comprehensive index permits quick scanning of the book as a whole.

The insight of Oliver Wendell Holmes Jr., distinguished Supreme Court justice, exemplifies the theme of the *Famous Trials* series. Taken from *The Common Law*, published in 1881, Holmes remarked: "The life of the law has not been logic, it has been experience." That "experience" consists mainly in how laws are applied in society and challenged in the courts, a process resulting in differing outcomes from one generation to the next. Thus, the *Famous Trials* series encourages readers to examine trials within a broader historical and social context.

Introduction

"I've Decided to Go Ahead"

O N FRIDAY, MARCH 19, 1971, reporter Neil Sheehan of the *New York Times* received copies of a top secret Defense Department study outlining the history of U.S. involvement in Vietnam. The Vietnam War was then in full swing, with no end to the conflict in sight. Sheehan received the documents, which came to be known as the Pentagon Papers, from Daniel

---

American troops in the Mekong Delta, Vietnam. The top secret Pentagon Papers detailed the history of U.S. involvement in Vietnam.

Ellsberg, a former Defense Department analyst who had come to be opposed to the war.

As Sheehan and other *Times* reporters pored over the massive study, a lively debate was sparked within the newspaper about the advisability of publishing stories based on the documents. Some inside the paper believed publication would be criminal and irresponsible, while others believed the *Times* had a responsibility to the public to print what it had learned.

The publisher of the *Times*, Arthur Ochs Sulzberger, was less than enthusiastic about publication. He was uneasy about publishing secret government material and said he would exercise his right to cancel the project at any time.

Other considerations also weighed heavily on the minds of *Times* executives. All the editors worried they might inadvertently publish material that would harm current military or intelligence operations in a conflict in which more than one hundred thousand American soldiers were directly involved. The paper's outside legal advisors warned the paper would be guilty of violating the federal Espionage Act if it published anything from the study and warned that simply having the document in its possession was illegal. By the end of May, Sulzberger still had not decided whether the paper would publish the material.

Perseverance by those such as Managing Editor A. M. Rosenthal and General Counsel James Goodale finally convinced Sulzberger that the *New York Times* had a responsibility to its readers to make the material public. Goodale knew the government likely would try to stop the *Times* from publishing the material through an injunction, a court order forbidding the paper from making the classified documents public. He also assumed the government would have a good chance at getting at least a temporary restraining order on publication. Goodale said he believed "a judge would sign a temporary restraining order ... simply because he would be afraid, as would any normal person, of the unknown" after having had the Defense Department study "dumped in his lap with 'top secret' marked on it."[1] But he also believed the newspaper could ultimately prevail.

A demonstration about the Pentagon Papers. The Pentagon Papers case brought forth the issue of freedom of the press versus the government's right to security.

Although Sulzberger had been unimpressed with Sheehan's early drafts of stories based on the documents, on June 11 he finally agreed to publication. Sulzberger called editors and other executives to his office and announced, "Gentlemen, I've decided to run only the documents and not the stories,"[2] a reference to earlier debates about whether the paper should only publish stories based on the study and not the documents themselves. The editors were dumbstruck, but Sulzberger had only been joking. "I've decided to go ahead the way you planned it,"[3] he said. The *Times* would publish a ten-part series, with a limit of six pages per day. The confrontation between the government of the United States and the *New York Times* would come to a head in less than three weeks.

Chapter 1

The First Casualty
of War

IT IS OFTEN SAID that the first casualty of war is truth. During wartime, governments have an interest in misleading their enemies, maintaining domestic morale, and rallying support for the nation's war effort. Propaganda, disinformation, and censorship are traditional tools used by governments to promote their goals during times of war. These methods, however, create a conflict between the government's need to keep secrets and the public's right, in a democratic society, to be told the truth.

Making the truth known, or at least gathering and publicizing information, is the role adopted by the press in the United States. Sometimes called the Fourth Estate, or fourth branch of government, the press reports on the activities of government officials, enabling citizens to make informed choices at election time and to protest what they consider unwise policies by elected officials. The press has sometimes been called a watchdog, scrutinizing the government's performance and exposing abuses of power.

Conflicting Interests Collide in Wartime

The role of the press is especially important in times of war. National debates about whether to enter into war, which could end up costing hundreds of thousands of lives and billions of dollars, have an enormous impact on the country's future and could even determine the nation's survival. However, public debate or detailed stories in the press about national security issues, such as battle plans or troop locations, could be disastrous, endangering the lives of men and women in the service. Stories critical of military efforts could dampen morale, reducing the likelihood of military success.

Conflicts between the government's need for secrecy and freedom of speech and the press have often emerged in the United States. In 1798, less than seven years after the ratification of the First Amendment to the Constitution, Congress passed what became known as the Alien and Sedition Acts. At the time, war with France seemed imminent. About twenty-five thousand French refugees then lived in the United States, some of whom were thought to be spies.

CONGRESS AND LAWS RESTRICTING FREE SPEECH

The plain words of the First Amendment appear absolute: "Congress shall make no law . . . abridging the freedom of speech, or of the press." However, seven years after the First Amendment was ratified, a Congress fearful of possible war with France passed the Sedition Act of 1798. The law gave the government broad authority to determine what type of speech and press reports would be allowed, and specified harsh penalties for those found guilty of sedition, or leading people to resist or rebel against the government.

Over the years 1798 and 1799, twenty-five people were arrested, fifteen or more were indicted, eleven were tried and ten found guilty of violating the sedition law. Among those found guilty were Matthew Lyon, a congressman from Vermont, who was jailed for four months and fined one thousand dollars for criticizing President Adams and his policy toward France. As related by constitutional scholar Irving Brant in his book *The Bill of Rights: Its Origin and Meaning*, Lyon had written to a newspaper that he would always feel free to speak out about what he perceived to be abuses of power by the president. Brant says Lyon wrote he would support any effort to promote the interests of the American people, but that he would not be supportive "whenever I shall, on the part of the Executive, see every consideration of the public welfare swallowed up in a continual grasp for power, in an unbounded thirst for ridiculous pomp, foolish adulation, and selfish avarice."

After becoming president, Thomas Jefferson pardoned all prisoners, including Lyon, convicted under the law, and Congress ultimately repaid all fines that had been collected. It would not be the last time, however, that the government would seek to suppress criticism.

President John Adams supported the Alien and Sedition Acts, passed in 1798.

The alien law, favored by President John Adams, gave the president power to expel noncitizens from the United States if they were found to be disruptive to the peace and safety of the nation. The sedition law, also championed by Adams, made it illegal to publish false, scandalous, or malicious writings against the government, Congress, or the president. Those found guilty of violating the sedition law could be fined up to two thousand dollars and put in prison for up to two years.

Censorship and Duty

Later, as tempers rose over the issue of slavery and national leaders feared the nation could splinter, censorship again became a common practice. In the 1830s laws prohibiting people from teaching slaves to read were made tougher, and President Andrew Jackson proposed that it be made illegal to send anti-slavery publications through the mail in the South. Congress imposed limits on the discussion of slavery within its chambers. After mobs in Boston and Philadelphia burned buildings and threatened those in favor of abolishing slavery, Edward Everett, the governor of Massachusetts, went so far as to call for an end to all discussion of the slavery issue. "All classes must be invoked to abstain from discussion, which by exasperating the master, can have no effect other than to render more oppressive the condition of the slave."[4]

When the issue of slavery finally erupted into the American Civil War in 1861, other limits on freedom of speech and the press were enacted. President Abraham Lincoln took control of northern telegraph offices as part of an effort to make sure they were not used to disseminate information that might weaken the Union war effort. As the war progressed and casualties mounted, a number of northern papers printed unflattering critiques of Lincoln. The government restricted circulation of some of those papers, seized all copies of others and jailed editors considered disloyal to the Union cause. Lincoln believed that, in conflicts between the military's need for secrecy and the press's need for freedom, the military must prevail during wartime. In 1864 he said the question was "between what was

The increasing amount of death and destruction as the Civil War progressed prompted criticism from newspapers.

due to the military service on the one hand and the liberty of the press on the other."⁵

Despite government censorship, press access to troops during the Civil War was nearly unlimited. Franc B. Wilkie, a newspaper reporter, said that one camp, in Cairo, Illinois, was overrun with journalists:

> You meet newspaper men at every step; they block up the approaches to headquarters; one of them is attached to the button of every officer; they are constantly demanding passes, horses, saddles, blankets, news, copies of official papers, a look into private correspondence and things whose use and extent are only appreciated by omniscience.⁶

Although Lincoln was willing to punish the press for reports he considered harmful to the Union war effort, he was not willing to impose "prior restraints" — legal efforts preventing the press

President Abraham Lincoln believed that during wartime, the military's need for secrecy took priority over the freedom of the press.

Union general William Tecumseh Sherman had reservations about allowing reporters access to the camps.

from publishing stories. As a result, journalists enjoyed broad freedom to gather and print information from the military.

"The World's Gossips"

In time, many military leaders would grow to resent and distrust the press. For example, Union general William Tecumseh Sherman, writing in his memoirs, said journalists accompanying troops "are mischievous. They are the world's gossips, pick up and retail the camp scandal, and gradually drift to the headquarters of some general, who finds it easier to make reputation at home than with his own corps or division."[7] Sherman also worried that military leaders, either through boasts of their own actions or through a mistake, might offer information that enemies could use for military advantage.

Despite his reservations, Sherman was resigned to the necessity of dealing with the press. "Yet, so greedy are the people at large for war news, that it is doubtful whether any army commander can exclude all reporters, without bringing down on himself a clamor that may imperil his own safety," Sherman wrote. "Time and moderation must bring a just solution to this modern difficulty."[8]

Time and moderation, however, are rare commodities in wartime. Speech that is perfectly acceptable during times of peace often is viewed with fear and suspicion when the nation is at war and world events are turbulent. For example, the Espionage Act, passed on June 15, 1917, provided for up to twenty years imprisonment and up to a ten-thousand-dollar fine for spoken or written opposition to World War I.

The Espionage Act was subsequently amended a year later to make it a crime to obstruct the sale of U.S. bonds by "uttering, printing, writing, or publishing any disloyal, profane, scurrilous, or abusive language, or language intended to cause contempt, scorn, contumely or disrepute"[9] to the form of government of the United States, the Constitution, the flag, or the uniforms of the Army and Navy. The amendment also made it illegal to say or write anything intended to cause resistance to the U.S. war effort, or in support of the nation's enemies. Violations of these provisions carried the same twenty-year jail sentence and ten-thousand-dollar fine.

A Difference Between War and Peace

About nine hundred people were convicted of violating the Espionage Act during World War I. One of the most famous cases involved Charles T. Schenck, who was the leader of the Philadelphia Socialist Party. In 1917, Schenck mailed more than fifteen thousand leaflets to men reported in newspapers as having passed draft board physical examinations. The leaflets urged the men to ignore the military draft, comparing conscription to slavery. Found guilty of violating the espionage law and given a six-month jail sentence, Schenck appealed to the U.S. Supreme Court.

The case reached the Court in 1919, providing the justices with their first opportunity to rule on the degree to which the government could limit expression. Schenck argued that although he intended to disrupt military recruitment, he was protected by the First Amendment. Writing for a unanimous Court, Justice Oliver Wendell Holmes Jr. rejected the claim. Adopting what would become known as the "clear and present danger" test, Holmes indicated that speech rights are not absolute but depend on the individual situation. "The question in every case is whether the words are used in such circumstances and are of such a nature as to create a clear and present danger that they will bring about the substantive evils that Congress has a right to prevent. It is a question of proximity and degree."[10]

THE AUTHOR OF THE "CLEAR AND PRESENT DANGER" TEST

Oliver Wendell Holmes Jr. was born into an aristocratic Boston family on March 8, 1841. He was named after his father, an anatomy professor at Harvard Medical School and a writer who socialized with such people as Henry Wadsworth Longfellow and Ralph Waldo Emerson. Groomed by his father to follow in his footsteps, the young Holmes nevertheless had decided by 1861 that he wanted to pursue a career in the law.

Holmes' father tried to sway his son, arguing, according to Liva Baker's *The Justice from Beacon Hill: The Life and Times of Oliver Wendell Holmes*, that the law was no career for a gentleman. Among other things, the elder Holmes said lawyers had only "recently emerged from a state of quasi barbarism."

Undeterred by his father's views, by 1867 Holmes was in practice in Boston. He went on to teach constitutional law at Harvard and lecture on common law at the Lowell Institute. His twelve Lowell lectures were published shortly before his fortieth birthday to worldwide acclaim.

Holmes was appointed to the Massachusetts Supreme Court in 1882, where he served for twenty years until selected by President Theodore Roosevelt on December 2, 1902, to serve on the United States Supreme Court. Holmes served on the Court for twenty-nine years, developing a reputation for examining each case on its own particular facts.

One of Holmes' most memorable First Amendment opinions came in the 1919 case of *Schenck v. United States*, in which a socialist activist distributed antiwar leaflets to military draftees. In upholding the man's conviction for violating the Espionage Act, Holmes announced what became known as the Court's "clear and present danger" test. Under that test, speech is not protected by the First Amendment if there is a strong chance it will cause illegal behavior —especially in wartime. As detailed in *Congressional Quarterly's Guide to the U.S. Supreme Court*, edited by Elder Witt, Holmes said, "When a nation is at war, many things that might be said in time of peace are such a hindrance to its efforts that their utterance will not be endured so long as men fight and that no Court could regard them as protected by any constitutional right."

Holmes retired from the Court on January 12, 1932, at the age of ninety-one. He died on March 6, 1935.

Franklin D. Roosevelt encouraged wartime reporting but retained the military's right to censor the articles.

Americans' free speech rights also were curtailed during World War II, but the government came to see the press as a potential ally in its effort to shape public opinion on the war. President Franklin Delano Roosevelt created the Office of Censorship and the separate Office of War Information. The censorship office was given the power to review news stories prior to publication and to remove information the military did not want made public. Decisions of the military censors could not be appealed. Despite the censorship, the volume of news increased during the war, in part because the government had come to encourage the reporting of the war.

A Gradual Flowering of Press Freedoms

Although the government could and did practice censorship, civil libertarians say free speech rights were protected to a much higher degree in World War II. In 1943, the American Civil Liberties Union reported:

The government has not resorted to prosecution or censorship on any appreciable scale. War-time prosecutions brought by the Department of Justice for utterances, and publications barred by the Post Office Department as obstructive, have so far numbered about forty-five, involving less than two hundred persons, compared with over a thousand persons involved in almost as many cases in World War I. Even though some of the proceedings were hardly justified by any reasonable interpretation of the "clear and present danger" test laid down by the Supreme Court, the Department of Justice has on the whole shown commendable restraint.[11]

"The Greatest Soldiers in the World"

By the time of the Vietnam War, the situation had changed again. There were no significant attempts to censor the press, and journalists freely traveled with troops. The press generally approached the war as patriotic supporters of the conflict, a point of view that clouded coverage and led journalists to accept the

The activities of American soldiers in Vietnam received more press coverage than they had in any previous war.

word of officials. Many critics of the press have charged that journalists were actually "cheerleaders" for the U.S. military effort in Vietnam, at least in the beginning.

On February 9, 1966, ABC reporter Dean Brelis provided a report on the ground war in which U.S. troops were lauded as "the greatest soldiers in the world. In fact, they're the greatest men in the world. . . . They came over here to win."[12] Reporters who covered the air war in Vietnam eagerly and unquestioningly accepted military reports about sophisticated weaponry and the professionalism of American soldiers and pilots.

Press Begins More Objective Reporting

As reporters' own observations proved many official military reports to be false, the press began to report the war with more objectivity. Official briefings in Saigon became known as the "follies," and reporters increasingly searched on their own for stories.

Two popular magazines, *Time* and *Life*, offer an example of the slow change in news coverage that occurred during the Vietnam War. During the early 1960s, the magazines rarely covered the war or region. Eventually, as the war escalated, the magazines opened a bureau in Saigon. Reporters' stories, however, were routinely softened by editors, who were influenced by reports from White House, State Department, and Pentagon officials.

Another change was in the attitude of reporters toward the war itself. By October 1967, the opinion of the magazines' owner, Hedley Donovan, had soured. An editorial in *Life* that month said that although the nation had entered Vietnam for "honorable and sensible purposes," the war was "not absolutely imperative"[13] to U.S. interests.

On January 30, 1968, the tone of news coverage turned to complete skepticism about statements made by military officials. That night, about seventy thousand communist soldiers launched an assault on South Vietnam's urban centers. Named the Tet Offensive because it coincided with the celebration of Tet, the lunar New Year, the string of simultaneous attacks

Refugees flee across a bridge over the Perfume River in Hue to escape the fighting during the Tet Offensive.

throughout South Vietnam was capped by the temporary occupation of the American embassy in Saigon. A little over six hours later, American troops had retaken the embassy, but the television images and newspaper accounts reinforced an already growing perception among the U.S. public that the Vietnam War was misguided and unwinnable.

Shortly after the Tet Offensive, CBS anchorman Walter Cronkite visited Saigon. Upon his return, Cronkite told viewers on February 27 that despite promises of victory from military officials, it seemed "more certain than ever that the bloody experience of Vietnam is to end in a stalemate."[14] Cronkite's report dismayed President Lyndon Johnson, who believed it would further erode public support for the war.

Despite the disappointment and hostility the Johnson Administration and Pentagon officials felt about the nature of the reporting from Vietnam after the Tet Offensive, no attempts were made to censor the work of reporters. In part this may have been due to the fact that the U.S. Congress had never formally declared war in Vietnam. As a result, the government had less legal basis for attempting to impose restrictions on the press. Years later, Chief Justice William H. Rehnquist noted, "Without question the government's authority to engage in conduct that infringes civil liberty is greatest in time of declared war."[15] Moreover, there were only a small number of cases in which the press breached security or endangered lives. Barry Zorthian, a spokesman for the American embassy in Vietnam, counted no more than five security breaches during a five-year period in which more than two thousand journalists were on the scene.

The Pentagon Papers Stir Move to Restrict Press

By 1971, the national mood was increasingly in favor of ending the Vietnam War. Street protests, many led by Vietnam veterans, were on the increase, and influential members of Congress urged President Richard Nixon to bring all U.S. troops home by

Veterans and reservists protest the Vietnam War. Protests increased as public support for the war dwindled.

the end of the year. Nixon refused to be swayed by the rising antiwar sentiment, saying that "while everybody has a right to protest peacefully, policy in this country is not made by protests."[16] The president did not, however, attempt to control the increasing calls in the press for a withdrawal from Vietnam.

Nixon would soon decide, however, that the press should be controlled. Nixon realized that the United States could not win the war and considered the press to be responsible. He complained, "More than ever before, television showed the terrible human suffering and sacrifice of war. . . . [T]he result was a serious demoralization of the home front, raising the question of whether America would ever again be able to fight an enemy abroad with unity and strength of purpose at home."[17] However, his change of thinking did not come about because of reporting on the scene in Vietnam, which by 1971 was reinforcing the general domestic dissatisfaction with the war. What prompted Nixon to act against the press was the disclosure of a Pentagon study that provided a history of U.S. involvement in Vietnam.

The study, which soon became known as the Pentagon Papers and ran to forty-seven volumes, included activities in Vietnam under the administrations of Presidents Harry S Truman, Dwight D. Eisenhower, John F. Kennedy, and Lyndon B. Johnson. Many of the documents within the study demonstrated that the U.S. government was more deeply involved in the Vietnamese civil war than officials ever indicated publicly.

On Sunday, June 13, 1971, the *New York Times* published stories and summaries of the Pentagon Papers, which were classified "Top Secret—Sensitive." The *Times* had received a copy of the study from Daniel Ellsberg, a former Pentagon analyst and consultant.

Publication of stories based on the Pentagon Papers would soon set in motion one of the most famous First Amendment cases ever to come before the U.S. Supreme Court. On June 30, just seventeen days after the *Times* first published articles based on the classified study, the Court issued its landmark ruling.

Chapter 2

A Threat to National Security

A T 10 A.M. ON SUNDAY, June 13, President Nixon met with White House Chief of Staff H. R. Haldeman, who kept thorough notes of all his meetings with the president. The conversation was wide-ranging. Nixon talked about the Rose Garden wedding ceremony the previous day of his daughter, Tricia, to Edward Finch Cox, and about continuing tensions between Pakistan and India. Nixon also commented on that morning's stories in the *New York Times* that were based on the Pentagon Papers.

Nixon told Haldeman the stories shed a bad light on the policies of President John F. Kennedy and said the stories would create difficulties in dealing with the government of South Vietnam. He added that it was "criminally traitorous" for the papers to have been leaked to the *Times* and for the *Times* to have published them. Still, Nixon believed the disclosures were not detrimental to his own administration. He told Haldeman "we need to keep clear of the *Times'* series."[18]

Later that day, however, Nixon changed his mind after a thirteen-minute phone call with then–National Security Adviser Henry Kissinger. Kissinger said, "the fact that some idiot can publish all of the diplomatic secrets of this country on his own is damaging to your image, as far as the Soviets are concerned, and it could destroy our ability to conduct foreign policy. If other powers feel that we cannot control internal leaks, they will never agree to secret negotiations."[19]

Nixon Decides to Act

By the following day, Nixon was ready to act. He asked Halde-man to get an assessment of the *Times*'s criminal liability for pub-lishing classified information and to find out who leaked the confidential report. He also told Haldeman to curtail the access of *Times* reporters to the White House.

Concern about the stories in the *Times* was also growing at the Justice Department. The second story in the series, published June 14, 1971, was headlined "Vietnam Archive: A Consensus to Bomb Developed Before '64 Election, Study Says." The story attracted the attention of Robert C. Mardian, assistant attorney general of the Justice Depart-ment's Internal Security Division. He contacted Attorney General John Mitchell, who agreed the Justice Department should examine the possibility of legal action and consider the possible national security consequences of the *Times* reports.

Mardian and Mitchell asked William H. Rehnquist, then the assistant attorney general in charge of the department's Office of

After speaking with Henry Kissinger (left), President Richard Nixon (right) determined that the Pentagon Papers were a threat to national security.

Legal Counsel, to examine the possibility of forcing the *Times* to stop publishing articles based on the Pentagon Papers by obtaining a legal injunction, or court order. Requesting such an order was a grave step. An injunction of this type would amount to a prior restraint on publication, and the Supreme Court, in a 1931 decision, in a case known as *Near v. Minnesota*, established broad protection for newspapers from prior restraints. The Court had, however, left open the possibility of their use in extreme circumstances.

Injunction Seen as Winnable

After reviewing the Court's *Near* decision, Rehnquist advised that, because of the ongoing Vietnam War, the government had a reasonable chance of getting an injunction against the *Times*. He also said the government's odds of winning would be greater if it could show national security would be harmed by further publication.

The Justice Department, however, was having a difficult time assessing the national security implications of the reports in the *Times*. No one at Justice had seen the study. Then, once officials received a copy, they were overwhelmed by the study's massive size. Looking for help from other agencies in making its case, the department turned to the State Department, where pressure from foreign governments had prompted Secretary of State William P. Rogers to complain to Mitchell that additional stories by the *Times* would be "inimical [adverse] to the national interest."[20]

William H. Rehnquist maintained that the government had a good chance of getting an injunction against the Times.

Justice also turned to the Defense Department. There, Fred J. Buzhardt, the department's general counsel, said the last four volumes of the Pentagon study, covering the diplomatic history of the war, would endanger national security if made public. Buzhardt's boss, Defense Secretary Melvin R. Laird, said the study included sensitive information whose disclosure would harm national defense.

Government Asks *Times* to Halt Publication

Mardian decided it was time to act. Meeting Monday night with Mitchell, Mardian helped draft a telegram to the *New York Times* asking the paper to voluntarily suspend publication of articles based on the Pentagon Papers. The telegram, sent in Mitchell's name, said:

> I have been advised by the Secretary of Defense that the material published in *The New York Times* on June 13, 14, 1971, captioned "Key Texts from Pentagon's Vietnam Study," contains information relating to the national defense of the United States and bears a top-secret classification. As such, publication of this information is directly prohibited by the provisions of the Espionage Law, Title 18, United States Code, Section 793. Moreover, further publication of information of this character will cause irreparable injury to the defense interests of the United States. Accordingly, I respectfully request that you publish no further information of this character and advise me that you have made arrangements for the return of these documents to the Department of Defense.[21]

Mardian called to warn the *Times* the government would seek an injunction against the paper if it did not voluntarily suspend publication. The telegram and phone call initially were debated among senior management officials at the *Times*. Some argued the paper had nothing to gain by further publication, while others said stopping publication would set a bad precedent for the press by appearing to cave in to government pressure.

Ultimately, *Times* publisher Arthur Ochs Sulzberger was consulted. Although he had been unenthusiastic about the series initially, Sulzberger listened to the advice of James Goodale, in-house lawyer for the *Times*, who told Sulzberger that "we cannot afford for the future of this newspaper to stop publication now. It would be terrible."[22]

"The Interest of the People"

Times editors then drafted a response to the Justice Department. It said:

> We have received the telegram from the Attorney General asking the *Times* to cease further publication of the Pentagon's Vietnam study. The *Times* must respectfully decline the request of the Attorney General, believing that it is in the interest of the people of this country to be informed of the material contained in this series of articles. We have also been informed of the Attorney General's intention to seek an injunction against further publication. We believe that it is properly a matter for the courts to decide. The *Times* will oppose any request for an injunction for the same reason that led us to publish the articles in the first place. We will of course abide by the final decision of the court.[23]

The following day, June 15, 1971, the *New York Times* published its third installment of stories about the study, this one detailing the way President Johnson had obtained permission to move ground troops into Vietnam. But the lead story in the *Times* that day was about the paper's legal scuffle with the Justice Department, which was headed for the courtroom.

About noon on June 15, Michael D. Hess entered Judge Murray I. Gurfein's courtroom in the federal courthouse near Foley Square in Manhattan. Hess, who was in charge of the civil division in the office of the U.S. Attorney for the Southern District of New York, was armed with legal papers drawn up overnight by Mardian and other Justice Department attorneys. His job that day would be extraordinary: For the first time in the

President Johnson meets with troops in Vietnam. One of the Times's *stories reported how Johnson got permission to send ground troops into Vietnam.*

nation's history, the federal government was asking a court to impose a prior restraint on the press.

A Violation of Espionage Laws Alleged

Hess told the court that the *New York Times*'s use of the Pentagon Papers violated federal espionage laws, laws which he said also gave federal judges authority to order the newspaper to stop publication. He conceded the government could launch a criminal proceeding against the *Times*, but said such a move, which in the meantime would allow the paper to continue publication of its series, would take a long time to prepare and would do nothing to compensate the government for harm to its national security interests. Hess said "serious injuries are being inflicted on our foreign relations, to the benefit of other nations opposed to our form of government," and said the *Times* should at the very least be required to endure a "slight delay"[24] in publication so the court could make a judgment.

Hess also told Gurfein a court injunction against the *Times* barring the paper from further publication was the only way to protect the government's interests adequately. The government had a right to the injunction, he said, because the Pentagon Papers properly had been classified top secret, meaning that their unauthorized disclosure could cause serious national defense problems. Hess also told Gurfein the *Times* had no right to possess or publish the study's contents, and that the newspaper's first three installments already had jeopardized national defense. More stories, he said, would injure the government further.

In support of his position, Hess noted Secretary of State Rogers's statement that several allies had expressed "concern over the disclosures in the articles."[25] Hess also gave Gurfein affidavits signed by Buzhardt and Mardian alleging harm to national security from publication of portions of the Pentagon Papers.

Government Optimistic

Gurfein, who had served in Army intelligence in World War II, told Hess he believed the government might win the case. By the time he completed his argument, Hess believed the *Times* would be restrained from further publication.

Representing the *New York Times* were Alexander Bickel, a Yale University law professor, and Floyd Abrams, a partner in a Wall Street law firm. Bickel argued that the Espionage Act was not drafted by Congress with the idea it would be used against newspapers. Calling the government action a "classic case of censorship,"[26] Bickel also claimed the government was overly vague in its request, failing to identify what portion of the espionage laws could possibly be used for its lawsuit.

Times: First Amendment Is Not Absolute

Bickel did make an important concession. He said there are circumstances under which a prior restraint could be imposed against a news organization without violating the First Amendment. Bickel quickly asserted, however, that the Pentagon Papers case was not one that required such a remedy.

A WINNING STRATEGY

Alexander Bickel, a law professor at Yale University, had only a very short time to prepare for arguments before the Supreme Court. One key question was whether he should argue that the First Amendment prohibits all prior restraints, an absolutist position, or whether he should take a more cautious approach by arguing that prior restraints are sometimes constitutional, but not in the case of the Pentagon Papers. In meetings with officials at the *New York Times*, he argued for a conservative course, believing the paper would fare better before the Supreme Court, where he thought the case ultimately would be decided.

As Bickel analyzed the backgrounds of the members of the Court, he believed the *Times* would have the votes of Justices Hugo Black and William O. Douglas, jurists who consistently had expressed strong support for the First Amendment. Bickel also believed Justices William J. Brennan and Thurgood Marshall would be against a prior restraint in the *Times* case. David Rudenstine, in his book *The Day the Presses Stopped: A History of the Pentagon Papers Case*, writes:

> But to prevail the *Times* needed a fifth vote, and Bickel said the *Times* would likely get that vote from either Justice Potter Stewart or Justice Byron White, both of whom considered the absolutist's position extreme and might be offended if the *Times* asserted it. He contended that the *Times*'s chances of ultimately persuading one or both of these justices to rule in its favor would be strengthened if the *Times* conceded that the government could enjoin publication in limited circumstances but insisted those circumstances did not exist in this case.

Although some *Times* officials believed the newspaper should take a stand against all prior restraints, a majority sided with Bickel. Throughout the course of the case, the *Times* conceded that prior restraints could be imposed on the press in certain circumstances, none of which applied to the newspaper's publication of Pentagon Papers stories. As Bickel had surmised, that concession ultimately would have an impact on the Supreme Court's ruling.

Gurfein suggested to Bickel that the *Times* consent to a temporary restraining order, which would allow the court several days to decide the issue on the basis of greater evidence and without unnecessary haste. Gurfein added pressure, saying he assumed "we are all patriotic Americans."[27] The implication was that the *Times* would be unpatriotic if it did not consent to the decree. But Bickel brushed the suggestion aside, arguing, "A newspaper exists to publish, not to submit its publishing schedule to the United States government."[28]

Gurfein later met privately with the lawyers for both sides in his chambers, and then issued his ruling. The *Times*'s protests notwithstanding, Gurfein imposed a temporary restraining order on the paper barring it from publishing any more articles based on the Pentagon Papers until he could hold a full hearing and issue a ruling.

A Question of "Irreparable Harm"

In his order, Gurfein said any harm resulting from the delay in publication "is far outweighed by the irreparable harm that could be done to the interest of the United States Government if it should ultimately prevail."[29] But Gurfein did not require the *Times* to turn over its copy of the defense study, saying that he did "not believe *The New York Times* will willfully disregard the spirit of our restraining order."[30] He ordered the two sides to appear for a full hearing on Friday, June 18.

The *Times* decided it would not appeal Gurfein's order, largely because Bickel and Abrams believed an appeal would be unsuccessful. The *Times* also decided to comply with the order. Bickel believed it was important for the *Times* to show respect for the legal process, especially since he thought the issue ultimately would be decided by the Supreme Court. Instead of another installment in the *Times*'s Pentagon Papers series, the newspaper on Wednesday carried a story about the granting of the temporary restraining order.

Later that day, one complete set of the Pentagon Papers was sent to the U.S. Attorney's Office in New York, while another was delivered to Judge Gurfein's chambers. Sending the copy to Gurfein turned out to be a mistake. No government official ever admitted to knowing who ordered that a copy be delivered to Gurfein, and Gurfein himself was puzzled. Because no security precautions had been established, Gurfein began to wonder whether the government's claims of a threat to national security were overstated.

Doubts About Damage to National Security

With the help of two assistants, Hess began studying the documents delivered to the U.S. Attorney's office. They hoped to find documents that would bolster their contention that additional disclosures in the *Times* would harm national security. But as they pored over the voluminous study, they came across newspaper articles and presidential speeches—items accessible to anyone—which were stamped top secret. They too began to have doubts about the seriousness of the threat the Papers held to national security.

By the time the two sides met in Gurfein's courtroom at 10 A.M. Friday, another newspaper, the *Washington Post*, had independently received its own copy of the Pentagon Papers. Up to that point, the *Post* had simply published articles based on material that had appeared in the *Times* and had given the *Times* credit. Friday's *Post* contained the paper's first installment of original reporting, an article exposing American attempts in 1954 to put off an election in Vietnam.

Hess and his boss, U.S. Attorney Whitney North Seymour Jr., were shocked when they learned of the *Post* story. Bickel opened his argument Friday by stating that the Pentagon Papers were continuing to appear in the press despite the injunction against the *Times*. As a result, he said, the government's request for a standing injunction against the *Times* was unnecessary. "This story is out," Bickel said. "Without any exaggeration, we can assume [that] this story . . . will be made available by every news medium in the United States to the public."[31] Bickel added that continuing the restraining order on the *Times* injured the paper because it was forced to stand idle while the *Post* published.

Fallout from the *Washington Post*

Gurfein turned to the government lawyers and asked whether the federal government intended to seek an injunction against the *Post*. Hess said he had been unaware of the *Post* story, but said it was irrelevant to the *Times* case. Because the Pentagon study was so large, he said, the government still had plenty of

The Times's *legal team argued that it was unfair and unnecessary to restrict the* Times *when other newspapers and the media at large would eventually report the same information.*

material to protect. He also chastised Bickel for claiming the injunction against the *Times* was unfair, saying the *Times* was solely responsible for its situation by "opening up the subject, being the first to announce that they were going to publish and coming into this court and asking this court to decide. . . . We would say that they put themselves in this unique position."[32]

Bickel angrily countered, "We are not in this court because we came . . . seeking its approval of our publishing enterprise. We are in this court because the Government brought us in this court." He also attacked the government's contention that further publication would harm the nation. "Another installment of that story has been published," he said. "The republic stands and it stood for the first three days."[33]

But Gurfein stepped in and told Bickel that a

> free and independent press ought to be willing to sit down with the Department of Justice and screen these documents that you have or [that] the *Washington Post* has or [that] anybody else has as a matter of simple patriotism to determine whether the publication of any of them is or is not dangerous to the national security.[34]

Hearing Closed to the Public

Later the government was given the chance to make its case. Seymour told Gurfein the case boiled down to a question of whether someone who "comes into possession of documents which have been classified under lawful procedures . . . may unilaterally declassify these documents in his sole discretion."[35] The government also offered a number of witnesses who provided general assertions that publication of portions of the Pentagon Papers by the *Times* had harmed national security interests and that further publication would cause greater harm. The witnesses would not offer more detailed descriptions in open court, but agreed to do so in a so-called *in camera* session, or one from which the public was barred.

During the closed session, Dennis J. Doolin, a deputy assistant secretary of defense for international security affairs, testified that, among other things, the Pentagon Papers included intelligence material that showed how the United States was able to intercept and decipher North Vietnamese messages. He said such a disclosure in the *New York Times* would destroy the ability of the United States to continue breaking the North Vietnamese code. Doolin also referred to secret efforts by foreign governments to intercede with North Vietnam to secure release of U.S. prisoners of war. He used Sweden as an example of one such government.

Doolin and other witnesses were under orders from Mardian and Buzhardt not to reveal specifics, even in closed session. When

Gurfein pressed for specifics, Doolin mistakenly said the Pentagon Papers had no documents outlining Sweden's involvement. "There is none?" Gurfein said. "Why did you mention Sweden then?"[36] Doolin assured Gurfein he was trying to be helpful, but got flustered as the judge became increasingly irritated.

A Ruling for the *Times*

The court was reopened to the public at 9:50 P.M., when Gurfein heard closing arguments, which ended after 11 P.M. The next afternoon, June 19, Gurfein issued an opinion in favor of the *Times*. "The security of the nation is not at the ramparts alone," Gurfein said. "Security also lies in the value of our free institutions. A cantankerous press, an obstinate press, a ubiquitous press must be suffered by those in authority in order to preserve the even greater values of freedom of expression and the right of the people to know."[37]

Gurfein said the government had not shown why publication by the press of the Pentagon study would affect the nation's security, and said the espionage law upon which the government hinged its case did not apply to newspapers. "This has been an effort on the part of the *Times* to vindicate the right of the public to know," he said. "It is not a case involving an intent to communicate vital secrets for the benefit of a foreign government or to the detriment of the United States."[38] Still, Gurfein continued the restraining order against the *Times*, prohibiting it from publishing while the government sought an appeal to the U.S. Court of Appeals for the Second Circuit.

Appeals court judge Irving R. Kaufman later that day continued the restraining order until all eight of the judges then sitting on the circuit could meet to consider the matter. On June 23, the appeals court reversed Gurfein's order and sent the matter back to Gurfein to determine whether items in the Pentagon Papers threatened a "grave and immediate danger to the United States."[39]

The *Washington Post* Joins the Fray

While the *New York Times* was arguing against the restraining order before Judge Gurfein, the *Washington Post* was making similar arguments before Judge Gerhard A. Gesell of the U.S. District Court for the District of Columbia. On June 18, Gesell held a short hearing before issuing an opinion in favor of the *Post*. The government immediately appealed to the U.S. Court of Appeals for the District of Columbia Circuit, which in the early morning hours of June 19 reversed Gesell's ruling and temporarily enjoined the paper from further publication of Pentagon Papers stories pending a fuller hearing on the matter by Gesell.

Gesell on June 21 held another hearing and again ruled in favor of the *Post*. The government again appealed, and received an extension of the temporary restraining order from the appeals court, which agreed to hear the case the following day. The appeals court on June 23 ruled in favor of the *Post*, but kept the restraining order intact in order to give the government a chance to appeal to the U.S. Supreme Court. The government did just that on June 24, while the *Times* that day also appealed its case to the high court.

On Friday, June 25, the nine Supreme Court justices voted five to four to continue the stays but also set a hearing to consider the *Times* and *Post* cases on an expedited basis. The Court set June 26 as the day it would hear arguments in the two cases.

Chapter 3

Government Warns of Wartime Complications

AFTER THE SUPREME COURT agreed to decide the Pentagon Papers dispute, the State Department and the Defense Department provided Solicitor General Erwin N. Griswold with a comprehensive list of materials that officials believed would cause disastrous results if published by newspapers. Griswold, the government's top courtroom lawyer, found the list too extensive and decided to narrow it.

Griswold was worried the government's case would be harmed if it claimed publication of almost anything from the Pentagon Papers would irreparably harm national security. He began studying the documents, but soon realized he would never be able to comb through the entire study prior to oral arguments in the case. Griswold called in three government experts to help identify sensitive materials: William Macomber Jr., a State Department official; Lieutenant General Melvin Zais, the director of operations for the U.S. military's Joint Chiefs of Staff; and Admiral Noel Gayler, director of the National Security Agency. "Look, tell me what are the worst, tell me what are the things that really make trouble,"[40] Griswold told the experts. The men came up with a list of forty-one items, which Griswold then looked up in the Pentagon Papers.

Griswold felt publication of most of the items cited by the officials would be more likely to be a cause of embarrassment to

SECRECY CONCERNS HAUNT THE GOVERNMENT

On November 5, 1953, President Dwight D. Eisenhower issued Executive Order 10501, which established the classification system for the executive branch of government. As related by Sanford J. Ungar in *The Papers and The Papers*, the order set up three categories of information whose distribution could be limited.

The designation of "top secret" was given to

information or material the defense aspect of which is paramount, and the unauthorized disclosure of which could result in exceptionally grave damage to the Nation such as leading to a definite break in diplomatic relations affecting the defense of the United States, and armed attack against the United States or its allies, a war, or the compromise of military or defense plans, or intelligence operations, or scientific or technological developments vital to the national defense.

The designation of "secret" was given to

defense information or material the unauthorized disclosure of which could result in serious damage to the Nation, such as by jeopardizing the international relations of the United States, endangering the effectiveness of a program or policy of vital importance to the national defense, or compromising important military or defense plans, scientific or technological developments important to national defense, or information revealing important intelligence operations.

Finally, the category of "confidential" was reserved for "defense information or material the unauthorized disclosure of which could be prejudicial to the defense interests of the Nation."

Under the order, documents were to receive the highest classification contained in any of its parts. For example, the Pentagon Papers included material that could be used to discern how quickly the United States military was able to decode messages of the North Vietnamese and as a result contained the designation of top secret. However, the Pentagon Papers also included newspaper articles, speeches and other material readily available to the public. Because those materials, even though part of the public domain, were included in a study with defense secrets, the entire Defense Department study was labeled top secret.

Even legal briefs detailing the government's security concerns about further publication of stories based on the Pentagon Papers were considered militarily sensitive. When Solicitor General Erwin Griswold filed his sealed brief with the Supreme Court, security agents were aghast that Griswold handed the brief to the Supreme Court clerk, who did not have a proper security clearance.

the government and to the governments of other countries than a true threat to national security. For example, the study divulged that Sweden, which was hosting anti–Vietnam War conferences and was publicly denouncing the U.S. role in the conflict, was actually serving as an intermediary between the United States and North Vietnam in an attempt to negotiate a peace settlement. Even the nation's chief Cold War foe, the Soviet Union, was involved in efforts to broker peace talks. Despite pressure from Attorney General Mitchell, Griswold whittled the list to eleven items, one of which encompassed four volumes of material relating U.S. attempts to negotiate a settlement in Vietnam and garner release of U.S. prisoners of war. It was in those volumes, which none of the newspapers possessed, that information about Sweden, the Soviet Union, and others was detailed.

A Veil of Secrecy

Two briefs (summaries of the legal arguments) would be required from each side. One would be available for anyone to read; the other would be sealed, or secret. Griswold had an assistant write the government's open brief for the court, then set about writing the government's secret, supplemental brief to be submitted to the Supreme Court's justices. A sealed brief was deemed necessary so the government could identify specific items from the Pentagon Papers whose disclosure would harm national security. Putting such information in an unsealed brief would allow anyone who requested to see briefs in the case to discover the secrets the government was going to such extraordinary lengths to conceal. The Defense Department was so concerned about keeping the information from the public that security officials from the Pentagon even complained that because Griswold's secretary did not have a security clearance, the solicitor general should get someone else to type the sealed brief. But Griswold asked the agents to leave his office and told them to report to their supervisors that "the Solicitor General of the United States will not follow your instructions."[41]

In the government's secret brief, Griswold warned that revelations from the four diplomatic volumes could lead some inter-

Marines depart Vietnam for home. Solicitor General Griswold claimed that further reporting on the Pentagon Papers would slow troop withdrawals from Vietnam.

mediaries between the United States and North Vietnam to stop participating, thereby reducing chances of an end to the war. In addition, Griswold said further news stories based on the Pentagon Papers could slow the rate of U.S. troop withdrawals from Vietnam, compromise activities by agents of the Central Intelligence Agency, and "make the enemy aware of significant intelligence successes," which could affect military operations because the ability to intercept and decipher military messages by the North Vietnamese "now gives direct support to our troops today, and saves many lives. It also helps, directly, in the recovery of downed pilots."[42]

The sealed brief concluded by emphasizing the government's view that the First Amendment is not absolute, meaning there are instances in which the right of the press to publish material must be weighed against the government's right to conduct negotiations and wage war. The government's sealed brief said:

In a proper allocation of powers, the courts should support the Presidency in a narrow and limited area where such protection is needed in the effective meeting of the President's responsibility, and in the safeguarding of American lives. This is not a question of exception to the First Amendment, but of rational interpretation of that provision wholly consistent with its history and purpose.[43]

A Narrow Issue

The open brief made clear that the government was no longer seeking to prohibit publication of all material from the Pentagon Papers. Rather, it was only trying to prevent certain portions of the study from being distributed. The government's open brief said:

The issue before the Court, although of great importance, is narrow. There is no question here of any blanket attempt by the Government to enjoin the publication of a newspaper, or any attempt to impose a generalized prohibition upon the publication of broad categories of material. The only issue is whether, in a suit by the United States, the First Amendment bars the Court from prohibiting a newspaper from publishing material whose disclosure would pose a grave and immediate danger to the security of the United States.[44]

The government dropped its reliance on alleged violations of the Espionage Act, a decision based at least in part on the fact that federal appeals courts had concluded the spy laws did not include specific authority for the government to stop newspapers from printing articles. The section of the espionage laws the government had relied upon made it a criminal offense to communicate information relating to national defense to people without proper authorization. The lower courts had decided that because Congress used the word "communicate" instead of "publish," the newspapers were not guilty of violating that section of the law. Instead of challenging that interpretation at the Supreme Court, the government decided to press another argument more forcefully than it had in the lower courts.

The government's open brief quoted American statesman Alexander Hamilton.

The government argued that the office of the president of the United States had "inherent powers" under the Constitution to block publication of material harmful to the national interest. The government was arguing that, because the Constitution placed foreign relations and the military among the president's duties, the president had to have the power to conduct those activities effectively even if the Constitution did not explicitly state those powers.

President Needs Power to Conduct Foreign Affairs

The government's open brief included a quotation from Alexander Hamilton from *The Federalist Papers*, a series of essays written by Hamilton, James Madison, and John Jay between 1787 and 1788 that provided interpretations of the newly drawn Constitution and arguments in favor of its adoption by the states:

> The circumstances that endanger the safety of nations are infinite, and for this reason, no constitutional shackles can wisely be imposed on the power to which the care of it is committed. This power ought to be coextensive with all the possible combinations of such circumstances. It ought to be under the direction of the same councils which are appointed to preside over the common defence.[45]

Hamilton believed the president, given authority over national defense, obviously needed to have power to carry out that function even if not specified in the new Constitution.

The government brief added:

> Obviously, in circumstances like those here, the only effective means of protecting the nation against the improper disclosure of military secrets is to enjoin their impending publication. To limit the President's power in this regard solely to punishment of those who disclose secret information would render the power meaningless: the harm sought to be prevented would have been irreparably accomplished.[46]

The government's brief added, "Relatively innocuous consequences today may develop into serious and sometimes virtually insolvable problems in the future."[47]

The government in its brief also reminded the justices that, in the only other time in U.S. history in which the Court had considered the issue of prior restraints against the press, the 1931 *Near v. Minnesota* case, the justices had found the First Amendment is not absolute. The Court in that case said the government was entitled to prevent the obstruction of military recruiting "or the publication of the sailing dates of transports, or number and location of troops."[48]

Nation's Security Needs Are Broad

The government brief further argued that the *Near* decision applied to more than just military recruiting and troop movements:

> These examples were merely illustrative, and obviously there are other items of information so vital to the security of the United States that their publication may be enjoined. The exception to the prohibition upon prior restraint recognized in *Near v. Minnesota*, surely covers material whose publication would pose, "a grave and immediate danger to the security of the United States."[49]

The government also noted that diplomatic relations by their nature require secrecy:

> In this subtle and difficult world of diplomacy, things are often said in confidence that will prove so embarrassing if disclosed that the mere threat of disclosure is enough to leave them unsaid. Sensitive negotiations often are carried on through people, who, if they knew their identity might be disclosed, would be unwilling to participate.[50]

The following morning, as Griswold submitted the government's open brief and its closed, supplemental brief to the Supreme Court clerk, lines had already formed outside. Law students, tourists, and the merely curious had queued up, hoping for one of the less than two hundred seats available to the public to witness arguments in the case. By the time arguments began, more than fifteen hundred people had assembled.

A Low-Key Start to a High-Profile Case

At 11 A.M., Chief Justice Warren E. Burger began the historic hearing as if it were any other. "We will hear arguments in 1873 and 1885, the *New York Times* against the United States and the United States against the *Washington Post* Company."[51] The numbers "1873" and "1885" were the docket numbers assigned to the cases by the Court's clerk. The government was given an hour to present its case, and after brief opening remarks Griswold launched into the heart of his argument. He said:

Supreme Court Chief Justice Warren E. Burger presided over the cases against the Times *and the* Post.

It is important, I think, to get this case in perspective. The case, of course, raises important and difficult problems about the constitutional right of free speech and of the free press, and we've heard much about that from the press in the last two weeks. But it also raises important questions of the equally fundamental and important right of the Government to function.

Great emphasis has been put on the First Amendment, and rightly so. But there is also involved here a fundamental question of separation of powers in the sense of the power and authority which the Constitution allocates to the president, as chief executive and as commander-in-chief of the Army and Navy. And, involved in that, there is also the question of the integrity of the institution of the presidency: whether that institution—of the three great powers under the separation of powers—can function effectively.[52]

According to Griswold, the case was a simple one if one believed that the press may never be subject to a prior restraint. "If we start out with the assumption that never—under any circumstances—can the press be subjected to prior restraints, never—under any circumstances—can the press be enjoined from publication, of course we come out with the conclusion that there can be no injunction here," Griswold said. Alluding to the Court's decision in the *Near* case, Griswold said such an assumption was erroneous, because "there is no such constitutional rule, and never has been such a constitutional rule."[53]

Griswold also argued that the government was entitled to win the case on the basis of copyright law, arguing that only the government had a right to publish government material. Offering the hypothetical example of a manuscript written by Ernest Hemingway, Griswold said:

In some way the press gets hold of it. Perhaps it is stolen. Perhaps it is bought from a secretary through breach of fiduciary responsibility, or perhaps it is found on the sidewalk. If the *New York Times* sought to print that, I have no doubt that Mr. Hemingway or now his heirs, next of kin, could obtain from the court an injunction against the press printing it.[54]

"An Immediate Grave Threat"

Griswold told the justices that disclosure of some materials from the Pentagon Papers would be hazardous to the nation's security, prompting a question from Justice Potter Stewart.

Stewart: "Your case depends upon the claim, as I understand it, that the disclosure of this information would result in an immediate grave threat to the security of the United States of America."

Griswold: "Yes, Mr. Justice."

Justice Potter Stewart questioned what kind of threat to national security the Pentagon Papers presented.

Stewart: "However it was acquired and however it was classified?"

Griswold: "Yes, Mr. Justice. But I think the fact that it was obviously acquired improperly is not irrelevant in the consideration of that question. I repeat, obviously acquired improperly."[55]

The idea that disclosure of material had to cause "immediate" harm to the country concerned Stewart and Justice Byron White, who questioned Griswold further. In response, Griswold told the Court that it would be inappropriate for the Court to create a rule that would allow prior restraints only if publication would result in "a war tomorrow morning, when there's a war now going on."[56] In Griswold's view, the concept of national security included negotiations for the release of prisoners, or efforts to produce a treaty to stop the proliferation of nuclear weapons. Griswold said:

> In the whole diplomatic area the things don't happen at 8:15 tomorrow morning. It may be weeks, or months. People tell me that already channels of communication on which great hope had been placed have dried up. I haven't the slightest doubt, myself, that the material which has already been published, and the publication of other materials, affects American lives, and is a thoroughly serious matter.[57]

In one exchange that would later prove to be important in the Court's decision making, Justice William J. Brennan asked Griswold whether it was not "correct that the injunctions so far granted against the *Times* and *Post* haven't stopped other newspapers from publishing materials based on this study or kindred papers?"[58] Griswold said he believed the material being published by other papers was based on the *Times* and *Post* series, an effort by other papers which he characterized as "all kinds of window dressing"[59] that did not reveal new material. Brennan followed up by asking if other newspapers had copies of the

Justice William J. Brennan asserted that if many newspapers had copies of the Pentagon Papers, injunctions against the Times *and the* Post *would be useless.*

Pentagon Papers. Griswold said he was uncertain, but noted, "There is a possibility that anybody has it."[60]

A Question of Tactics

The idea that "anybody has it" was disturbing to Brennan, who said that, if multiple copies of the Pentagon Papers were circulating at newspapers across the country, an injunction against the *New York Times* and the *Washington Post* would be ineffective. Griswold responded that "there is nothing in this record, or known outside the record, which would indicate that this injunction would be useless."[61]

Justice White suggested to Griswold that the government had made a tactical error in choosing to seek an injunction. In White's view, the government should have brought a criminal case.

But Griswold replied by pointing out the importance of barring publication. "I find it exceedingly difficult to think that any jury would convict or that an appellate court would affirm a conviction of a criminal offense for the publication of materials which this Court has said could be published,"[62] Griswold said.

The Courts as Censors

Justice Thurgood Marshall openly worried that, if the government were to prevail, similar situations would occur requiring the Court's attention. Marshall said to Griswold:

> Mr. Solicitor General, what particularly worries me at this point is that I assume that if there are studies not now being made, in the future there will be studies made about Cambodia, Laos, you name it. If you prevail in this case, then in any instance that anybody comes by any of those studies, a temporary restraining order will automatically be issued. Am I correct?[63]

Griswold was uneasy with such a hypothetical question, telling Marshall he was unable to provide a blanket answer. But he added, "I think that if properly classified materials are improperly acquired, and that it can be shown that they do have

Justice Thurgood Marshall worried that ruling in favor of the government would turn the court into a "censorship board."

an immediate or current impact on the security of the United States, that there ought to be an injunction."[64]

Marshall was dissatisfied with Griswold's answer. He said accepting the government's approach would turn the federal court system into a "censorship board." In response to Marshall, Griswold said, "That's a pejorative [negative] way to put it, Mr. Justice. I don't know what the alternative is."[65] The exchange prompted an extended dialogue between the justices and Griswold.

Justice Hugo L. Black: The First Amendment might be.

Griswold: Yes, Mr. Justice. And we are, of course, fully supporting the First Amendment. We do not claim, or suggest, any exception to the First Amendment. And we do not agree with [lawyers for the newspapers who say] we have set aside the First Amendment, or that Judge Gesell or the two Courts of Appeals in this case have set aside the First Amendment by issuing the injunctions which they have.

The problem in this case is the construction of the First Amendment. Now, Mr. Justice Black, your construction of that is well known, and I certainly respect it. You say that "no law" means "no law," and that should be obvious.

Black: I rather thought that.

Griswold: And I can only say, Mr. Justice, that to me it is equally obvious that "no law" does *not* mean "no law." And I would seek to persuade the Court that that is true.[66]

Griswold concluded the government's argument by asking the Court to require the lower courts to provide a full-scale hearing on whether further disclosure of material from the Pentagon Papers would endanger national security. It was now time for the justices to hear from lawyers for the *New York Times* and the *Washington Post*.

Chapter 4

The *Times* Disputes Government Authority

B ECAUSE OF THE COMPRESSED time schedule required by the Supreme Court's agreement to hear arguments, lawyers for the newspapers had been as rushed as Griswold had been in preparing. Lawyers for the *New York Times* and the *Washington Post* had to produce both public and sealed briefs between Friday afternoon and Saturday morning, the day the Court would sit for oral arguments.

In its public brief, the *Times* reiterated the position it took before the lower courts, that the First Amendment cast doubts on, but did not absolutely prohibit, prior restraints on the press. The *Times*'s Alexander Bickel believed it would have been harmful to the newspapers' case to argue that the United States Constitution forbids all prior restraints. Later Bickel recalled,

> I think to have argued this case on the basis of an absolute position would have been foolish to the point of being almost unprofessional, so far as safeguarding the interest of my client was concerned. If you go into these cases with an ideological interest, like the American Civil Liberties Union, you've got nothing to gain but your ideology and nothing to lose but your ideology; then you have the luxury of an absolutist position. . . . I had to win a case.[67]

The *Times* stressed in its brief that the government had to demonstrate clearly why a prior restraint was justified before a court should allow an injunction. The *Times*'s brief said:

Prior restraints fall on speech with a brutality and a finality all their own. Even if they are ultimately lifted, they cause irremediable loss, a loss in the immediacy, the impact of speech. They differ from the imposition of criminal liability in significant procedural respects as well, which in turn have their substantive consequences. The violator of a prior restraint may be assured of being

"I THOUGHT ABOUT THE FIRST AMENDMENT"

James Goodale, general counsel for the *New York Times*, was only in his mid-thirties when the newspaper obtained a copy of the Pentagon Papers. The *Times*'s outside legal counsel, headed by Louis M. Loeb, who had been advising the paper since 1929, and Herbert Brownell, a former U.S. attorney general, strongly urged the newspaper's management not to publish, arguing that to do so would be irresponsible and a violation of federal law.

Goodale, however, believed it would have been irresponsible not to publish the material. Goodale's dogged insistence led to a classic Supreme Court confrontation between the government and the *New York Times*. Goodale recalled the battle in an interview on the Public Broadcasting Corporation's *Frontline*, a public affairs show. Transcripts of the interview, a portion of which follows, are available on the World Wide Web.

Question: What was your instinct when suddenly you're faced with this dilemma that the newspaper asks you about?
Goodale: With respect to the Pentagon Papers, you have to look at the law. That is to say the law that you can read in the case books. Then you have to ask about the law that you don't read about in the case books, the First Amendment. Because the First Amendment isn't attached to the Pentagon Papers espionage statute. You have to look at the statutes and then ask yourself constitutionally can you nonetheless print, at least in this country.
Question: What caused [you] to sort of give such weight to the bible of human rights over the other law?
Goodale: I was lucky because I had been at the *New York Times* for a period of 8 years before the Pentagon Papers came along. . . . I learned about the First Amendment in real life and then I began to teach myself the constitutional law as applied to the newsroom. So I was lucky. I thought about the First Amendment.

held in contempt. The violator of a statute punishing speech criminally knows that he will go before a jury, and may be willing to take his chance, counting on a possible acquittal. A prior restraint therefore stops more speech, more effectively. A criminal statute chills. The prior restraint freezes.[68]

Bickel and the *Times* then analyzed the government's contention that the president has the authority to seek prior restraints in order to fulfill his obligations in conducting foreign policy and serving as commander in chief of the armed forces. The *Times* said the president had no such power without statutory approval, except perhaps when national security is imperiled significantly. However, the newspaper said that, even if the justices were to accept as true all that the government said about the security implications of further disclosure of the Pentagon Papers, the nation was not in an emergency situation.

Espionage Law Does Not Apply to Newspapers

The *Times* also maintained that the portion of the espionage laws the government had cited in lower courts as the basis for their action did not apply to newspapers. According to the *Times*'s brief, an analysis of the espionage laws clearly showed that "when Congress wanted to proscribe the act of publishing as well as communicating, delivery or transmitting, it knew how to do so and insisted on doing it with precision."[69]

The *Times* concluded its brief by noting the strained nature of the relationship between the press and government. The newspaper's brief said, "Press and government have a curious, interlocking, both cooperative and adversary relationship,"[70] adding:

It is not a tidy relationship. It is unruly, or to the extent that it operates under rules, these are unwritten and even tacit ones. Unquestionably, every so often it malfunctions from the point of view of one or the other partner to it. The greater power within it lies with the government. The press wields countervailing power conferred upon it by the First Amendment. If there is something near a balance, it is an uneasy one. Any redressing of it at the expense of the press, as this case demonstrates, can come only at the cost of incursions into the First Amendment.[71]

It is not known what the *Times*'s sealed brief said. Following oral arguments before the Court, security agents seized all copies. Although the agents also seized all copies of the *Washington Post*'s sealed brief, which was subsequently declassified, the government has said the *Times*'s sealed brief cannot be located.

"Tilting at Windmills"

The *Post*'s sealed brief was scathing. It said the government's arguments were "utterly devoid of any credible evidence of a threat to national security" and said the government was "tilt[ing] at windmills."[72] The paper's public brief was more measured, arguing that prior restraints could be imposed only when the government can show an immediate threat to the nation's security.

The *Post* also said the government's earlier reliance on espionage law was misguided and quoted an amendment to the Espionage Act, passed in 1950, to support that contention. "Nothing in this Act shall be construed to authorize, require, or establish military or civilian censorship in any way to limit or infringe upon freedom of the press or of speech as guaranteed by the Constitution of the United States." The *Post* added that, even if the espionage law specifically authorized the president to seek a prior restraint on publication by newspapers of sensitive information, Congress does not have the power under the Constitution to, "by legislation, set aside the mandate of the First Amendment."[73]

After Griswold made his case to the justices on Saturday, June 26, it was Bickel's turn. Bickel began the *Times*'s presentation by noting that "no great alarm sounded"[74] when the newspaper launched its series on June 13, indicating the government's claim of a threat to national security was exaggerated. Hardly had

OTHER NEWSPAPERS PICK UP WHERE *TIMES* LEFT OFF

By Tuesday, June 22, 1971, both the *New York Times* and the *Washington Post* were under court orders barring them from publishing stories based on contents of the so-called Pentagon Papers, a massive Defense Department study outlining the history of U.S. involvement in the Vietnam War. However, stories would soon begin to appear in other newspapers across the country.

On June 22, the *Boston Globe* published a story headlined "Secret Pentagon Documents Bare JFK Role in Vietnam War." The government, however, rushed and got an injunction against the *Globe* preventing it from further publication of Pentagon Papers stories.

The next day, however, the *Chicago Sun-Times* launched its own series of stories. The government did not seek a restraining order against that paper. On June 24, the *Los Angeles Times* and the Knight newspaper chain—with newspapers in Detroit; Miami; Tallahassee; Akron; Boca Raton, Florida; Philadelphia; Charlotte; and Macon, Geogia—came out with their own version of stories based on the Pentagon Papers. No legal action was taken against those papers or against the *Baltimore Sun*, which published an article based on the study on June 25. The government did act, however, against the *St. Louis Post-Dispatch*, which also ran a Pentagon Papers story June 25. The *Post-Dispatch* was restrained on June 26, the same day the Supreme Court was hearing oral arguments in the *Times*'s and *Post*'s cases.

When the Boston-based *Christian Science Monitor* and the Long Island, New York, *Newsday* published Pentagon Papers stories on June 29 and June 30, respectively, however, the government took no action against those papers.

Assistant Attorney General Robert Mardian, who initially spearheaded the government's efforts against the *Times* and *Post*, said the government looked at two factors in determining whether to seek legal action against newspapers. As quoted in Sanford J. Ungar's *The Papers and The Papers*, Mardian said decisions on whether to seek injunctions were based on answers to two questions: "Had the newspaper published information from a classified document, the disclosure of which could cause irreparable harm to the United States and which had not been previously in the public domain? Was [the newspaper] intending to continue publication?"

Bickel begun, however, when Chief Justice Burger cut in, asking whether it was not appropriate for all sides to step back so that lower courts could properly examine the material to ensure the nation's security was preserved.

Government Had Adequate Time to Make a Case

Bickel replied that the government actually had been given ample time to air its views. He noted that Judge Gurfein, during closed hearings, had attempted to "provoke from the Government witnesses something specific, to achieve from them the degree of guidance that he felt he needed in order to penetrate this enormous record." He said Gurfein "got very little, perhaps almost nothing,"[75] but all the while the government never made a formal request for more time.

Bickel also reiterated the *Times*'s position that the First Amendment does not bar all prior restraints. He told the Court: "We concede—we have all along in this case conceded—for purposes of the argument, that the prohibition against prior restraint, like so much else in the Constitution, is not an absolute. But beyond that . . . our position is a little more complicated than that."[76]

In elaboration, Bickel said that because the government's request for a prior restraint was not based on a law, such as the Espionage Act, the government was relying on a legal theory of "an inherent Presidential power." He said that although the president did have authority to establish a classification system for documents that was binding on the executive branch of government, that authority did not extend to seeking a prior restraint of the press except in the most serious of national emergencies. According to Bickel, such an emergency existed only when publication of materials would create "a mortal danger to the security of the United States." He said a prior restraint was appropriate only when it was clear on reading the material in question that "the public safety is an issue."[77]

"Death of a Hundred Young Men"

Justice Harry A. Blackmun then asked whether the certain death of soldiers would satisfy Bickel's proposed test for when a prior restraint was appropriate. Bickel said the high court's *Near* decision made clear, through its example of the hypothetical publication of the location of a troop ship, that preventing deaths was a solid basis for imposing a prior restraint on the press. However,

Justice Harry Blackmun (pictured) questioned the Times's *lawyer Alexander Bickel on what necessitated prior restraint.*

Bickel said, prior restraints were never appropriate when the perceived harm of publication was in the diplomatic realm, adding that, in his view, the government had not shown that any material from the Pentagon Papers would lead to the death of soldiers.

Justice Stewart then tried to get Bickel to flesh out his position through the use of a hypothetical question.

Stewart: Now, Mr. Bickel, it's understandably and inevitably true that in a case like this, particularly when so many of the facts are under seal, it's necessary to speak in abstract terms.

Bickel: Yes, sir.

Stewart: But let me give you a hypothetical case. Let us assume that when the members of this Court go back and open up this sealed record, we find something there that absolutely convinces us that its disclosure would result in the sentencing to death of a hundred young men whose only offense had been that they were nineteen years old and had low draft numbers. What should we do?

Bickel: Mr. Justice, I wish there was a statute that covered it.[78]

Stewart noted that there was not a statute covering such a situation, and Bickel repeated his contention that nothing in the Pentagon Papers would lead to such a situation. Stewart, however, pressed on, demanding an answer of Bickel. Bickel was still uncomfortable with the question, responding, "I would only say as to that that it is a case in which in the absence of a statute, I suppose most of us would say—"[79]causing an exasperated Stewart to demand a response.

Stewart: Well, there isn't, we agree—or you submit—so I'm asking you in this case, what should we do? You would say the Constitution requires that it be published and that these men die. Is that it?

Bickel: No. No, I'm afraid I'd have, I'm afraid that my, the inclinations of humanity overcome the somewhat more abstract devotion to the First Amendment, in a case of that sort.[80]

William O. Douglas, one of the Supreme Court justices who heard the Pentagon Papers case.

Justices William O. Douglas and Hugo Black were troubled by Bickel's assertion that a prior restraint would be more defensible had Congress authorized the president to seek them to protect national security. Bickel responded, "We don't face it in this case and I really don't know. I'd have to face that if I saw it—if I saw the statute—if I saw how definite it was."[81]

"Congress Shall Make No Law ... "

With this response, Black became animated. "Why would the statute make a difference? Because the First Amendment provides that 'Congress shall make no law abridging freedom of the press.' And you can read that to mean Congress may make 'some laws' abridging freedom of the press?"[82] Bickel attempted to back away from the position Black had inferred.

> Bickel: No, sir—only in that I have conceded for purposes of this argument that some limitations, some impairment of the absoluteness of that prohibition, is possible. And I argue that whatever that may be—whatever that may be—it is surely at its very least when the

president acts without statutory authority, because that inserts into it, as well as separation of powers.

Black: That's a very strange argument for the *Times* to be making, that the Congress can make all of this illegal by passing laws.

Bickel: Well, I didn't really argue that, Mr. Justice. At least I hope not.

Black: That was the strong impression you left in my mind.[83]

Burger then entered the questioning, asking Bickel to consider another issue. Burger noted that another case, *Branzburg v. Hayes*, was pending before the Court. At issue in that case was whether the First Amendment shielded reporters from having to identify news sources before grand juries conducting a criminal investigation. Bickel was more than familiar with the case; he had written a friend-of-the-court brief for news organizations in the case. Burger questioned how the press could demand confidentiality of news sources when it was, in effect, denying the government that right in the Pentagon Papers case. Bickel said that,

Justice Hugo Black (pictured) questioned Bickel on his interpretation of the First Amendment.

despite an "appearance of unfairness,"[84] the issues were different because reporters refusing to identify sources were promoting the values of the First Amendment.

William R. Glendon, representing the *Washington Post*, then got his turn before the justices. Glendon began by arguing the lower court had correctly decided in the *Post* case that, in order for a prior restraint to be issued, the government had to show that publication would result in "irreparable injury to the United States."[85]

"A Hard Case"

Stewart again brought up the hypothetical situation involving the potential death of one hundred men, to which Glendon responded, "that is a hard case you put."[86] But in Glendon's view, "the government has not yet brought anything like that case to your Honors, nothing like that. What we have heard . . . is much more in the nature of conjecture and surmise."[87]

Burger asked Glendon how the government could possibly show that publication of certain materials would lead to irreparable harm to the nation. Glendon responded:

> Your Honor, I think if we are to place possibilities or conjecture against suspension or abridgment of the First Amendment, the answer is obvious. The fact, the possibility, the conjecture of the hypothesis, that diplomatic negotiations would be made more difficult or embarrassing, does not justify—and this is what we have in this case, I think, it's all we have—does not justify suspending the First Amendment.[88]

Glendon added, "I think maybe the Government has a case of the jitters here. But that does not warrant the stopping [of] the press on this matter."[89]

Glendon then went on to assert that the government had been given more than adequate time to make its case, making light of the government's contention that the lower courts should be required to undertake a more thorough examination of the issue. He said the government's position was nothing more than asking for "one more time, just one more time" on the hope that "maybe we can find something"[90] if given that extra opportunity. Glendon also expressed displeasure with the government's document classification system, under which entire volumes of material had to be given top secret status even if only one document within those volumes legitimately carried a top secret classification.

Government Made "Extravagant Claims"

According to Glendon, the Pentagon Papers were merely a history, and were titled as such. He said disclosure of the papers could not possibly threaten national security, arguing that the government was guilty of making "extravagant claims"[91] about the sensitive nature of the material.

Burger, who earlier had chastised Bickel about the press's seeming inconsistency in demanding to protect the identity of its sources without being willing to acknowledge the government's need for confidentiality, now took aim at Glendon. He wanted to know how the *Washington Post* could possibly expect the Court to be sympathetic to it in the Pentagon Papers case when newspapers were unwilling to divulge their sources. Glendon responded that it was the government that had initiated the court proceedings seeking an injunction, not the newspapers. "You were brought in," Burger said. Glendon responded, "We were brought in kicking and screaming."[92] The interchange between the two men continued.

> Burger: You are now in the position of making demands on the First Amendment . . .

> Glendon: That's right.

> Burger: And you say the newspaper has a right to protect its sources, but the government does not?

> Glendon: I see no conflict, Your Honor. I see no conflict at all. We're in the position of asking that there not be a prior restraint, in violation of the Constitution, imposed

Chief Justice Warren Burger claimed that the press did not recognize the government's need for confidentiality.

on us. . . . We are also in the position of saying that under the First Amendment we are entitled to protect our sources. And I find—frankly, I just don't find any conflict there, Your Honor.[93]

The People's Interests

Next, White indicated he was surprised by the newspaper's position that nothing in the forty-seven-volume Pentagon Papers was worthy of a top secret classification. Glendon said the burden of proving whether any such documents existed was the government's, adding, "Now it may be that the government would feel that the courts should delve into this pile of paper, forty-seven volumes, on its own from time to time, when the government is so moved that the courts should work for them."[94]

Glendon then summarized the *Post*'s position, asserting that "the interests of the United States are the people's interests." He added:

And you're weighing here—and this is why, I suppose, we're here—you're weighing here an abridgment of the First Amendment, the people's right to know. And that may be an abstraction, but it's one that's kept this country and made it great for some two hundred years, and you're being asked to approve something that the government has never done before. We were told by the attorney general to stop publishing this news. We didn't obey that order, and we were brought into court, and we ended up being enjoined.[95]

The argument before the Supreme Court ended at 1:13 P.M., and the justices immediately went into private deliberations. Although the newspapers had hoped for a ruling Saturday, they would have to wait until Wednesday, June 30, for the Court's resolution of the case.

Chapter 5

The Supreme Court Speaks as One—and Individually

SIX WEEKS PRIOR TO hearing arguments in the *Times* case, the Supreme Court had decided another important prior restraint dispute, *Organization for a Better Austin v. Keefe*. In that case, the Court ruled that a temporary injunction against publication of handbills unconstitutionally abridged speech and press freedoms.

The organization had been angry about the methods a real estate agent used to entice white homeowners to sell their homes to blacks, accusing the agent of an unethical practice known as "blockbusting." The agent vehemently denied the claims, so the organization began distributing circulars in the agent's neighborhood chastising his business practices. The agent was able to secure an injunction against the group, prohibiting further distribution. But the Supreme Court said the handbills were similar to a newspaper, adding "the injunction, so far as it imposes prior restraint on speech and publication, constitutes an impermissible restraint on First Amendment rights."[96]

Although a strong defense of press freedom and a defeat of government-imposed prior restraints, the *Keefe* case differed from the *Times* dispute because no national security issues loomed. Those were the issues that were particularly troubling to some of the justices.

"I've Seen Things That Shake Me"

After hearing oral arguments in the Pentagon Papers case June 26, a number of justices looked through the secret documents, which had been delivered to the Court. The documents were sealed and under guard. Justice Stewart read through the documents and emerged with concerns about the series in the *Times* and the *Post*. "I've seen things that shake me," he told his clerks. "There is no question that there is some stuff in there that could get people killed, and I hope it never gets out."[97] Still, Stewart was not certain whether publication by the *Times* would have a seriously adverse effect on national security.

Other justices saw nothing that gave them pause. Justice Douglas, for example, said he saw nothing of consequence in the Pentagon study. Douglas said "most of the 'facts' disclosed in the Pentagon Papers were so well known in Vietnam that only a newsman's decision (or his paper's decision) to look the other way and parrot what the military told him, kept the American public from knowing full well what was going on there, at least during the sixties."[98] And Justice Black believed there was no need to even look at the papers. A First Amendment absolutist, Black believed every newspaper article was constitutionally protected. Before the case even reached the Court, he discussed the issue with his clerks over dinner at his home. He said he "was never too fond of injunctions against newspapers." His wife asked whether he felt the same way when national

Supreme Court Justice Hugo Black was a firm believer in First Amendment protection of news articles.

security was involved. "Well, I never did see how it hurts the national security for someone to tell the American people that their government lied to them,"[99] Black replied.

Following oral arguments, the justices gathered to discuss the case. Chief Justice Burger said the government should have another opportunity to prove national security was jeopardized by the series in the *Times* and *Post*, and said the case should be returned to the lower courts for more hearings. He complained the cases had been handled too quickly, on what he termed a "panic basis."[100] Black and Douglas said the newspapers should be allowed to proceed with publication of the series. Justice John Marshall Harlan complained the Court had moved too quickly, but said he was prepared to vote for the government in the case. Justice Blackmun sided with the government, saying that the *Times* was "reprehensible" for publishing the stories, adding he had "nothing but contempt for the *Times*."[101] Justice Brennan favored the newspapers, and Justice Marshall was leaning in that direction as well.

Justices Stewart and White Key to Ruling

As Bickel had expected at the outset of the case, Justices Stewart and White proved to hold the key votes. Stewart was troubled

Justice John Marshall Harlan favored the government in the Pentagon Papers case.

over the case. Unlike Black and Douglas, who saw no situations in which the government could prevent newspapers from publishing articles, Stewart believed there were circumstances that might warrant a prior restraint. The issue for him was whether the government had proved that further publication of material from the Pentagon Papers would damage the nation's security, and he was not certain whether the government had succeeded or not.

White, too, believed prior restraints could sometimes be necessary, but he was not sure the Pentagon Papers case presented such an example. White did believe the government could prosecute the newspapers for printing classified material, but wanted more time to think the case over.

An Injunction in St. Louis Tips the Balance

In early deliberations, four justices favored the newspapers, three favored the government, and two, Stewart and White, were undecided. The turning point for the undecided justices came when the Court learned that a federal judge had enjoined the *St. Louis Post-Dispatch* from publishing stories based on the Pentagon Papers. Injunctions against the *Times* and *Post* were, in effect, useless because other newspapers obviously had obtained copies of the study. That was the issue that had concerned Brennan during oral arguments. Stewart and White decided to rule in favor of the newspapers.

Because a majority was in favor of lifting the ban immediately, it was imperative that the ruling be issued as soon as possible. Burger decided that instead of assigning a justice to write an opinion for the majority, as was the usual practice, the Court would issue a brief per curiam, or unsigned, ruling. Brennan was given the task of writing the *per curiam* ruling. Each justice would then write a separate opinion explaining his rationale for voting the way he had.

On June 30, just four days after hearing arguments in the case, the Supreme Court issued its ruling. The brief order began by describing how the case arrived at the Court, then continued with a quote from a 1963 censorship case, *Bantam Books, Inc. v.*

Sullivan. "Any system of prior restraints of expression comes to this Court bearing a heavy presumption against its constitutional validity,"[102] the order said. It continued:

> The Government "thus carries a heavy burden of showing justification for the imposition of such a restraint." *Organization for a Better Austin v. Keefe*, 402 U.S. 415, 419 (1971). The District Court for the Southern District of New York in the *New York Times* case, 328 F. Supp. 324, and the District Court for the District of Columbia Circuit, 446 F.2d 1327, in the *Washington Post* case held that the Government had not met that burden. We agree.[103]

Newspapers Free to Publish Pentagon Papers Stories

In the concluding paragraph, the Court dissolved the stays that had prevented the papers from continuing their series. The three-paragraph order appeared to provide the press with a major victory. Many questions remained, however. The Court, for example, said there is a "heavy presumption" against the use of prior restraints, and that the government had a "heavy burden" in trying to impose them on the press. But the order offered no guidance on what circumstances might justify the imposition of prior restraints against the press. But in the individual opinions of the justices a clearer picture emerges of what prior restraints might be permissible.

Black's opinion, which Douglas joined, provided the most expansive view of the First Amendment's free press protections. Black wrote:

> I believe that every moment's continuance of the injunctions against these newspapers amounts to a flagrant, indefensible, and continuing violation of the First Amendment. . . . In my view it is unfortunate that some of my Brethren are apparently willing to hold that the publication of news may sometimes be enjoined. Such a holding would make a shambles of the First Amendment.[104]

BLACK'S SILENT EDITOR

Justice Hugo Black was the author of one of the most widely quoted lines in the Supreme Court's Pentagon Papers case ruling. As recorded in *Constitutional Law: Volume II*, edited by legal scholars Norman Redlich and Bernard Schwartz, Black stated his view that only a free press can uncover government misconduct. He then said, "And paramount among the responsibilities of a free press is the duty to prevent any part of the government from deceiving the people and sending them off to distant lands to die of foreign fevers and foreign shot and shell."

As originally written, Black's famous line, according to David Rudenstine's *The Day the Presses Stopped: A History of the Pentagon Papers Case*, read: "And paramount among the responsibilities of a free press is the duty to prevent any part of the government from deceiving the people and tricking them into a war where young Americans will be murdered on the battlefield." Black shared the draft with his wife, Elizabeth, who thought the word "murdered" too strong. Black wrestled with the wording for hours, then woke Elizabeth at 4 A.M. He asked what she thought of the phrase sending American boys "to die of foreign fevers and foreign shot and shell," which he had culled from a Southern drinking song, "I Am a Dirty Rebel." Elizabeth pronounced the revised phrase "great."

Tracing the history of the Constitution and the adoption of the First Amendment, Black said it was clear to him that there were no circumstances under which the government could prevent the press from distributing news, regardless of where that news came from. He wrote:

In the First Amendment the Founding Fathers gave the free press the protection it must have to fulfill its essential role in our democracy. The press was to serve the governed, not the governors. The Government's power to censor the press was abolished so that the press would remain forever free to censure the Government. The press was protected so that it could bare the secrets of government and inform the people. Only a free and unrestrained press can effectively expose deception in government. And paramount among the responsibilities of a free press is the duty to prevent any part of the government from deceiving the people and sending them off to distant lands to die of foreign fevers and foreign shot and shell. In my view, far from deserving condemnation for their courageous reporting, the *New York Times*, the *Washington Post*, and other newspapers should be commended for serving the purpose that the Founding Fathers saw so clearly. In revealing the workings of government that led to the Vietnam war, the newspapers nobly did precisely that which the Founders hoped and trusted they would do.[105]

Prior Restraints Disfavored Under Constitution

In his opinion, Douglas, joined by Black, restated his long-held view that the First Amendment is an absolute bar to government restrictions on the press. He went on to note that no law prohibited the press from publishing the sorts of materials the *Times* and *Post* were using. The espionage law the government had relied upon said that anyone with unauthorized access to national defense information who "willfully communicates" the information for the benefit of foreign nations is subject to fines and prison time.

Justice William O. Douglas believed that the government had no right to restrict the press.

Douglas said the word "communicates" is not the same as "publication" by a newspaper. He said the law contains eight sections on espionage and censorship, and the word "publish" was specifically used in three of them. "Thus it is apparent that Congress was capable of and did distinguish between publishing and communication in the various sections of the Espionage Act,"[106] Douglas said.

In his written opinion, Brennan also indicated a distaste for prior restraints. He took pains to express his belief that "our judgments in the present cases may not be taken to indicate the propriety, in the future, of issuing temporary stays and restraining orders to block the publication of material sought to be suppressed by the Government."[107] Brennan said the lower courts in the *Times* and *Post* cases felt it necessary to impose restrictions on the press while the matter moved to the Supreme Court. But now that the Court had decided the matter, he said, it was clear that "the First Amendment stands as an absolute bar to the imposition of judicial restraints in circumstances of the kind presented by these cases."[108]

Speech Rights Reduced in Wartime

Brennan left open the possibility that prior restraints on the press could be tolerated in extremely limited circumstances. Noting decisions in the 1919 *Schenck* case, in which the Court said certain speech may be suppressed when the nation is "at war," and in the 1931 *Near* case, when the Court said the government could prevent publication of the sailing dates of transports, Brennan said those exceptions were not in evidence in the Pentagon Papers case. He pointed out:

> Even if the present world situation were assumed to be tantamount to a time of war, or if the power of presently available armaments would justify even in peacetime the suppression of information that would set in motion a nuclear holocaust, in neither of these actions has the Government presented or even alleged that publication of items from or based upon the material at issue would cause the happening of an event of that nature.[109]

In sharp contrast to the strong free-speech positions of Black, Douglas, and Brennan, Stewart and White indicated they were close to allowing injunctions against the papers but found that Congress had not passed a law specifically allowing the government to seek restraints on the press. Stewart, for example, said the presidency, which is responsible for international diplomacy and national defense, must be entitled to confidentiality and secrecy to undertake its duties successfully.

In Stewart's view, shared by White, the only way to provide checks and balances on the large powers of the presidency in a nuclear age was to have "an enlightened citizenry." He added that "without an informed and free press there cannot be an enlightened people."[110] Stewart knew that the values of a powerful presidency and an independent, free press would come into conflict and said that when they do, the presidency should win. The only reason he could not rule for the government in the *Times* case, he said, was because Congress had not enacted a specific law giving the government authority to prohibit publication of top secret materials by newspapers. Moreover, the fact that other newspapers had obtained copies of the supposedly secret documents persuaded both Stewart and White that the secrecy issue was irrelevant.

"Substantial Damage to Public Interests"

White, in particular, said he was bothered by some of the material contained in the Pentagon Papers, believing that "revelation of these documents will do substantial damage to public interests." However, he said the government had not provided the proof necessary to receive an injunction against the papers, "at least in the absence of express and appropriately limited congressional authorization for prior restraints in circumstances such as these."[111]

Although White, who was joined by Stewart, said he was unable to support a prior restraint in the Pentagon Papers case in the absence of a law authorizing such restraint, he noted the government always had the option of seeking a criminal prosecution against the newspapers for violating espionage and security laws. White then provided the government with a primer on how to carry out such a prosecution.

Marshall, too, was troubled by the lack of specific authorization for prior restraint. Although he said he agreed the president has broad authority to conduct international relations and military actions, he believed it would be unconstitutional for courts to intervene without an explicit law giving them such authority.

"The Constitution provides that Congress shall make laws, the President execute laws, and courts interpret laws," Marshall said. "It did not provide for government by injunction in which the courts and the Executive Branch can 'make law' without regard to the action of Congress."[112]

Disgust with "Unwarranted" Haste

Three justices who ruled outright against the newspapers decried the haste with which the courts had been compelled to handle the case. "An issue of this importance should be tried and heard in a judicial atmosphere conducive to thoughtful, reflective deliberation, especially when haste, in terms of hours, is unwarranted in light of the long period the *Times*, by its own choice, deferred publication,"[113] Burger wrote.

Referring to the fact that the *Times*, after receiving the documents, studied them for several months prior to publishing stories based on their contents, Burger said the *Times*, "presumably in its capacity as trustee of the public's 'right to know,' has held up publication for purposes it considered proper and thus public knowledge was delayed." He continued:

> No doubt this was for good reason; the analysis of 7,000 pages of complex material drawn from a vastly greater volume of material would inevitably take time and the writing of good news stories takes time. But why should the United States Government, from whom this information was illegally acquired by someone, along with all the counsel, trial judges, and appellate judges, be placed under needless pressure? After these months of deferral, the alleged 'right to know' has somehow and suddenly become a right that must be vindicated [immediately].

> Would it have been unreasonable, since the newspaper could anticipate the Government's objections to release of secret material, to give the Government an opportunity to review the entire collection and determine whether agreement could be reached on publication?[114]

Burger also took sharp aim at the *Times* for accepting the documents at all. "To me it is hardly believable that a newspaper long regarded as a great institution in American life would fail to perform one of the basic and simple duties of every citizen with respect to the discovery or possession of stolen property or secret government documents," Burger said. "That duty, I had thought—perhaps naively—was to report forthwith, to responsible public officers. This duty rests on taxi drivers, Justices, and the *New York Times*."[115]

Blackmun also was troubled by the speed with which the case was handled. In Blackmun's view, the press did not have a right to be free of all prior restraints, just as the government did not have an absolute right to impose those restraints to protect national security. Blackmun believed the issue was much too complex to be decided in so short a time. "What is needed here is a weighing, upon properly developed standards, of the broad right of the press to print and of the very narrow right of the Government to prevent."[116]

Time Necessary for Responsible Action

Harlan's opinion also criticized the pace of the proceedings. After tracing the development of the case, he said, "The frenzied train of events took place in the name of the presumption against prior restraints created by the First Amendment. Due regard for the extraordinarily important and difficult questions involved in these litigations should have led the Court to shun such a precipitate timetable."[117]

As Harlan saw it, the case involved a series of questions. First, does the Espionage Act authorize the government to bring these suits? Second, does the First Amendment allow federal courts to prohibit publications on national security grounds? Third, can publication of secret documents be prohibited simply because the government is harmed by the breach of security? Fourth, would disclosure of any information in the Pentagon Papers actually harm national security? Fifth, what deference should be given to administration officials in assessing the third and fourth questions? Harlan also wanted to know whether newspapers can keep and use documents they know were stolen. Finally, he wanted to know whether threats to national security outweigh the Constitution's presumption against prior restraints.

Harlan, joined by Burger and Blackmun, said the answer to these questions could only come with fuller hearings, and he saw no reason to move nimbly. "I cannot believe that the doctrine prohibiting prior restraints reaches to the point of preventing courts from maintaining the status quo long enough to act responsibly in matters of such national importance as those involved here."[118]

Justice Blackmun maintained that the case was too complex to be handled quickly.

A Qualified Victory

The Court's ruling was hailed as a ringing endorsement of free press rights. A. M. Rosenthal, managing editor of the *New York Times*, exulted, "This is a joyous day for the press—and for American society. Certainly the Justice Department was slapped down in its efforts to ask the courts to enjoin newspapers, and will not likely take that route again."[119]

However, only two justices—Black and Douglas—indicated unqualified support for the newspapers' position. Brennan believed the press was entitled to broad protection, but said there were times when stories might be prevented by government. White, Stewart, and Marshall agreed that the papers should be allowed to proceed, but did not take strong stands in defense of a free press. Moreover, two justices indicated they might have been willing to uphold criminal sanctions against the newspapers, meaning the newspapers' victory was less triumphant than Rosenthal's enthusiastic statement would indicate.

Chapter 6

Legacy of the
Pentagon Papers Case

REACTION TO THE SUPREME Court's ruling was swift and jubilant at newspapers. Rosenthal, managing editor of the *New York Times*, declared it "a glorious day. We won it. We've all won it. We've won the right to print." Rosenthal's counterpart at the *Washington Post*, Eugene Patterson, jumped on top of a desk and announced, "We win, and so does *The New York Times*."[120] The following day both papers immediately began publishing articles from their respective series based on the Pentagon Papers.

A rally outside the federal courtroom in Los Angeles during the trial of Daniel Ellsberg and Anthony Russo.

Reaction at the White House to the ruling was less than enthusiastic. The president's spokesman, Ronald Ziegler, brushed off reporters' requests for a response to the ruling, saying, "There is really no need for him [Nixon] to issue a statement on this. The President's view on the First Amendment is well known."[121] The next day, Attorney General

GOVERNMENT MISCONDUCT IN THE
TRIAL OF DANIEL ELLSBERG

On June 28, 1971, two days before the Supreme Court issued its opinion in the Pentagon Papers case, the Justice Department obtained an indictment against Daniel Ellsberg charging him with violations of the federal Espionage Act. Soon after Pentagon Papers stories began appearing in the *New York Times*, government officials speculated Ellsberg had provided the newspaper with the documents.

Ellsberg had been an enthusiastic supporter of the Vietnam War, helping to write a portion of the Pentagon Papers and serving as a civilian liaison for the American embassy in Vietnam. But by 1967, Ellsberg began to believe the war was fruitless. Working at the Rand Corporation, a defense-oriented civilian research institute, Ellsberg gained access to the entire study. Ellsberg made photocopies which he eventually provided to the *Times* and other newspapers, thinking the public would demand an end to the war if it saw how the government had managed the war effort.

Following the Supreme Court's ruling in the *Times* case, and as the government prepared its case against Ellsberg, President Richard Nixon decided it was necessary to set up a White House unit to learn as much as possible about Ellsberg. Nicknamed "the Plumbers" because its job ostensibly was to stop government leaks, the unit included as members Charles Colson, special counsel to Nixon, and E. Howard Hunt, a former agent for the Central Intelligence Agency.

In *The Right and the Power*, Watergate special prosecutor Leon Jaworski details the lengths to which the Plumbers were willing to go in order to discredit Ellsberg:

> On July 28, 1971, Hunt wrote a memorandum to Colson entitled "Neutralization of Ellsberg." "I am proposing a skeletal operations plan aimed at building a file on Ellsberg that will contain all available overt, covert and derogatory information," he said. "This basic tool is essential in determining how to destroy his public image and credibility." One of the suggestions in the memo was: "Obtain Ellsberg's files from his psychiatric analyst." Dr. Lewis Fielding of Beverly Hills had been Ellsberg's psychiatrist in 1968 and 1969. On July 26, two days prior to Hunt's memo, he had refused to be interviewed by the FBI regarding Ellsberg.

Revelations of a break-in of Fielding's office and of wiretap recordings of Ellsberg's telephone conversations would eventually lead the judge presiding over Ellsberg's trial to dismiss the charges on May 11, 1973.

John Mitchell said the government "was continuing to investigate the leaking of the Pentagon Papers," promising "to prosecute anyone who had broken the law."[122] The government attempted to prosecute Daniel Ellsberg, the man who had leaked the Pentagon study to newspapers, and Anthony Russo, who helped Ellsberg.

Paul McMasters, First Amendment ombudsman at the Freedom Forum in Arlington, Virginia, says the Court's decision was an important step in safeguarding press freedoms.

> The most important thing about the Pentagon Papers case was the court's refusal to cross the prior restraint line even for an issue of national security. The Pentagon Papers case is a terrific endorsement of what we often only pay lip service to. The decision set a very high standard for the government in trying to get a prior restraint.[123]

Prior Restraints Sometimes Allowed

Still, the Court had not completely ruled out the possibility of prior restraints. Moreover, as the litigation of the Pentagon Papers case itself showed, the government was able to obtain at least a temporary restraining order against publication of certain materials. In addition, the Court's ruling indicated only that the government had not met its "heavy burden" of justifying a prior restraint in that particular case. Although viewed as an important First Amendment ruling, *New York Times v. United States* by no means settled the issue of prior restraints once and for all.

Just five years after the Pentagon Papers case, the issue of prior restraints again surfaced in *Nebraska Press Association v. Stuart*, a dispute arising from a brutal multiple-murder trial in Sutherland, Nebraska. The underlying facts of the case virtually ensured widespread press interest in the case: an unemployed handyman was accused of multiple counts of rape and murder in the killing of a girl and five other members of her family. To preserve the defendant's right to a fair trial, a gag order had been placed on the press prohibiting journalists from reporting on testimony and evidence in a preliminary hearing in the case. The state district court judge in the case believed widespread media interest in the proceedings would make it difficult to assemble an impartial jury in the case.

The Nebraska Press Association appealed to the Nebraska Supreme Court, which modified the order to prohibit reporting only of confessions or facts that strongly implicated the accused of having committed the murders. Dissatisfied with that ruling, the association appealed to the U.S. Supreme Court. After the Court heard oral arguments in the case, the only split between the justices was on whether solely to overturn the Nebraska Supreme Court ruling and remove the order, or to make their ruling wider and prohibit all such gag orders. In the end, the Court stopped short of banning all gag orders, but sent a strong signal that the high court would not tolerate them in most instances.

A Clash Between the First and Sixth Amendments

The Court's ruling, in *Nebraska Press Association v. Stuart*, written by Burger, acknowledged the difficult issues involved in the case, pitting the constitutional rights of the accused against the constitutional rights of the press. The Constitution's Sixth Amendment guarantees the right to trial "by an impartial jury." A well-publicized case, however, could make it difficult to find a jury that did not have preconceptions about the accused's guilt or innocence. The question, then, was how to balance competing rights under the Constitution.

As Burger put it, "The authors of the Bill of Rights did not undertake to assign priorities as between First Amendment and Sixth Amendment rights, ranking one as superior to the other." He added that

> if the authors of these guarantees, fully aware of the potential conflicts between them, were unwilling or unable to resolve the issue by assigning to one priority over the other, it is not for us to rewrite the Constitution by undertaking what they declined to do. It is unnecessary, after nearly two centuries, to establish a priority

PRIOR RESTRAINTS DISPUTES
CONTINUE TO ARISE

Although the Supreme Court's ruling in the Pentagon Papers case reaffirmed a judicial distaste for prior restraints, the issue continues to arise in a variety of contexts. In August of 1999, the *Los Angeles Daily Journal* was temporarily enjoined from publishing a story about a lawsuit that had been mistakenly unsealed. California law provides that some insurance-fraud case files be sealed for sixty days in order to allow prosecutors time to evaluate whether to file criminal charges. A clerical error unsealed a case record on August 11, and a reporter for the Los Angeles paper discovered it.

The newspaper had anticipated publishing a story on August 13, but prosecutors obtained an injunction August 12 from Superior Court judge Victor Chavez. A day later Superior Court judge Reginald Dunn refused to lift the order. But on August 16, Dunn reconsidered and lifted the ban. The *Daily Journal* published its story on the following day. If the newspaper had disobeyed the ban, it could have been found in contempt of court and reporters and editors placed in jail.

Even though the U.S. Supreme Court ruled in 1971 that government had a heavy burden in justifying prior restraints even in cases of alleged threat to national security, the *Daily Journal* in 1999 found itself restrained from publication about a court case for three days.

applicable in all circumstances. Yet it is clear that the barriers to prior restraint remain high unless we are to abandon what the Court has said for nearly a quarter of our national existence and implied throughout all of it.[124]

The opinion made clear that there are other methods of protecting the rights of the accused without abandoning the First Amendment. For example, the trial's venue can be changed, the trial itself can be postponed and jurors can be sequestered and insulated from news coverage of the trial.

"The H-Bomb Secret"

Another illustration of the inconclusive disposition of the Pentagon Papers case came in a 1979 dispute, *United States v. Progressive, Inc.*, which again raised substantial questions of national security. The case arose when *Progressive* magazine attempted to publish an article titled "The H-Bomb Secret: How We Got It,

Why We're Telling It." The story was written by Howard Morland, a freelance writer without advanced scientific or technical training. The point of the article was to show that information crucial to the construction of atomic weapons is not as secret as the government claims. Morland scoured physics textbooks, magazine articles, unclassified government documents, and scientific reference books. He said he wanted to discover "as much as it is legal to know—and possible for a layman to understand—about thermonuclear design."[125]

Progressive's editorial staff also believed the article could provide the public with information that would help them accurately evaluate government policies behind the nuclear arms race with the Soviet Union. The editors believed government claims of a need for secrecy were unfounded since so much information could be compiled from information readily available to the layman.

The magazine's editors sent Morland's article to nuclear experts to ensure accuracy. One of the copies, however, was referred to the Department of Energy, which told the magazine it should not publish the material. When *Progressive*'s editors indicated they planned to go ahead with publication, the government sued the magazine to prohibit release of the article.

"A Grave Threat to Peace"

The government filed a number of affidavits in the case, including a statement by Secretary of State Cyrus Vance. Vance warned that publication of Morland's article would help other nations develop their own nuclear weapons, which would "irreparably impair the national security of the United States, and pose a grave threat to the peace and security of the world."[126]

Although the magazine produced experts who asserted that the information contained in the article was widely available even to those who do not have access to classified documents, federal district court judge Robert Warren restrained the publication of *Progressive*'s April issue. Warren said that although freedom is a precious commodity, "one cannot enjoy freedom of speech, freedom to worship or freedom of the press unless one first enjoys the freedom to live."[127]

In Warren's view, the article could be beneficial to some nations in accelerating their weapons programs, a development that could lead to a nuclear war. "Faced with a stark choice between upholding the right to continued life and the right to freedom of the press, most jurists would have no difficulty in

THE SUPREME COURT AND UNPOPULAR EXPRESSION

The flag of the United States of America has become a potent symbol. Supporters of the country see in its stars and stripes the shared struggle and national sacrifice necessary to build a great nation. Critics see in the same flag stains left by corporate greed and political corruption.

Because of its potency as a national symbol, the flag often has been incorporated into speech. In 1984, Gregory Lee Johnson burned an American flag as part of a political protest outside the Republican National Convention in Dallas. Johnson was convicted of desecrating a venerated object in violation of Texas law. The Court of Appeals for the Fifth District of Texas affirmed the conviction, but the Texas Court of Criminal Appeals overturned it. The U.S. Supreme Court, on a five-to-four vote, also sided with Johnson on June 21, 1989.

Writing for the majority, Justice William J. Brennan said Texas was trying to punish Johnson solely because the state found his message objectionable. Consequently, the state law was unconstitutional. "If there is a bedrock principle underlying the First Amendment, it is that the government may not prohibit the expression of an idea simply because society finds the idea itself offensive or disagreeable," Brennan wrote in an opinion that may be found on the Internet at http://laws.findlaw.com/US/491/397.html.

According to Brennan, protecting the flag through restrictive laws does the flag and the ideals for which it stands no justice. Brennan explains,

The way to preserve the flag's special role is not to punish those who feel differently about these matters. It is to persuade them that they are wrong. We can imagine no more appropriate response to burning a flag than waving one's own, no better way to counter a flag burner's message than by saluting the flag that burns, no surer means of preserving the dignity even of the flag that burned than by— as one witness here did—according its remains a respectful burial. We do not consecrate the flag by punishing its desecration, for in doing so we dilute the freedom that this cherished emblem represents.

opting for the chance to continue to breathe and function as they work to achieve perfect freedom of expression," Warren said. He said that if he erred by ruling against the government, the way may be paved "for thermonuclear annihilation of us all."[128]

The magazine appealed the ruling to the United States Court of Appeals for the Seventh Circuit, but while the case was pending similar information appeared in a letter to the *Madison Press Connection*. The case became irrelevant, and it remains unclear how the appeals court, or ultimately, the Supreme Court, would have ruled in the matter.

A Decent Interval

A year later, the high court did get an opportunity to rule on another important First Amendment case, *Snepp v. United States*. Frank Snepp, a former CIA analyst in Vietnam who had been awarded the agency's Medal of Merit, returned to the United States following the Vietnam War disillusioned with the CIA and its role in the conflict. He left the agency to write a book, *Decent Interval*, in which he criticized the CIA's performance in Vietnam. Like all CIA employees, Snepp had signed a contract when he joined the agency under which he agreed to submit any writings about his CIA experiences to prepublication review by the agency. Snepp, however, did not allow the CIA to review *Decent Interval* prior to publication on the grounds that it did not contain any classified information.

The Justice Department brought Snepp to court, alleging a breach of his prepublication agreement. The U.S. District Court for Eastern Virginia ruled that Snepp had violated his contract and ordered him to provide the government with all earnings from the book. Snepp won a partial victory on appeal, but the government brought the matter to the Supreme Court. Although the government was willing to concede, for the sake of argument, that Snepp did not utilize any classified material in the book, the Court found that Snepp had permanently waived his First Amendment rights when he signed the agency contract. "The government has a compelling interest in protecting both the secrecy and the appearance of confidentiality so essential to the effective operation of our foreign intelligence service,"[129] the Court said.

Moreover, the Court held the government's interest was so important that, even without a signed contract, the CIA could require prepublication review. In the Court's view, "even in the absence of an express agreement, the CIA could have acted to protect substantial government interests by imposing reasonable restrictions on employee activities that in other contexts might be protected by the First Amendment."[130]

Manuel Noriega and Prior Restraints

In 1990, the U.S. war on drugs provided federal courts with yet another opportunity to consider the issue of prior restraint. The year before, the United States had managed to arrest Panamanian dictator Manuel Antonio Noriega on charges of drug trafficking. Noriega was taken under guard to Miami, Florida, and held at the Metropolitan Correctional Center there to await trial. Under the facility's policy of monitoring telephone calls of all inmates, the correctional center made tapes of Noriega's conversations with his lawyers. Cable News Network, which never has revealed how it did so, obtained seven of the recordings.

Instead of going on-air immediately with the tapes, CNN representatives went to the offices of the head of Noriega's legal team, Frank Rubino. They played the tapes for Rubino, who identified the voices. CNN told the lawyer that the network

Panamanian dictator Manuel Noriega was arrested in 1989 on drug trafficking charges.

planned to report about the tapes on a November 8 broadcast. On November 7, Noriega's defense team filed a motion to prevent CNN from using the tapes on the grounds that Noriega's right to a fair trial and his attorney-client privilege would be violated if CNN aired the material.

On November 8 federal district judge William M. Hoeveler, who was to preside over Noriega's criminal trial, ordered CNN to give him the tapes so he could rule on Noriega's request. He also imposed a restraining order on the network barring it from using the tapes until he could decide the matter. Instead of complying, CNN filed an appeal to the U.S. Court of Appeals for the Eleventh Circuit. On November 10, the appeals court affirmed Hoeveler's ruling, prompting CNN to ask the Supreme Court to review the matter. Eight days later, the Court by a seven-to-two vote denied the request. Justices Thurgood Marshall and Sandra Day O'Connor in dissent said the lower court rulings were in direct conflict with the high court's decision in the *Nebraska Press* case.

Since the Supreme Court had declined to intervene, the network was compelled to provide Hoeveler with the tapes, who then had a transcript made, translating Noriega's conversations from Spanish into English. Hoeveler reviewed the transcripts, found nothing in them that would take away from Noriega's rights, and lifted the restraining order on CNN. Although in the end CNN was allowed to air the material, the network nevertheless was under a prior restraint for twenty days, a dramatic demonstration that the press must sometimes fight to vindicate its rights—notwithstanding a Constitution that guarantees freedom to the press and a wealth of favorable Supreme Court rulings.

Limiting Access

During the Persian Gulf War in 1990 and 1991, the nation's bitter Vietnam experience would manifest itself in a starkly different Pentagon approach to media relations. Whereas journalists enjoyed nearly unlimited access to battles and officers during the war in Vietnam, the media would be tightly controlled during the

Journalists covering the Persian Gulf War were allowed limited access to combat areas, and their articles were subject to military review.

Persian Gulf War. The Defense Department drew up a list of regulations covering the type of information it considered suitable for release to the media. For example, the regulations prohibited reporters from detailing specific numbers of troops or their locations or details about search and rescue operations while they were ongoing.

The Pentagon rules also set up a system of press pools, which were small groups of reporters who were given limited access to combat areas. The pools were chaperoned by military personnel while in the field, and upon their return from the battlefield the reporters were required to share the information they had received with other reporters in the pool system. The system greatly reduced the number of newspeople in the field: although there were more than 1,600 journalists sent to cover the Gulf War, only about 160 were allowed anywhere near the fighting. Stories written by pool reporters were subject to military review, although the rules did not provide for a strict censorship of reports. If military officials and reporters could not come to agreement about a particular report, the regulations stated that the reporter's news organization would be allowed to decide whether to print the information in question. That portion of the rules said:

> In the event of hostilities, pool products will be subject to review before release to determine if they contain sensitive information about military plans, capabilities, operations, or vulnerabilities . . . that would jeopardize the outcome of an operation or the safety of U.S. or coalition forces. Material will be examined solely for its conformance to the attached ground rules [establishing the bounds of acceptable reporting], not for its potential to express criticism or cause embarrassment. The public affairs escort officer on scene will review pool reports, discuss ground rule problems with the reporter, and in the limited circumstances when no agreement can be reached with a reporter about disputed materials, immediately send the disputed materials to [other military officials] for review. . . . The ultimate decision on publication will be made by the originating reporter's news organization.[131]

Premeditated Censorship

Although there was little censorship of pool reports—of the more than thirteen hundred pool reports filed, only one story, detailing intelligence operations, was modified—many in the press complained bitterly about the pool system. Chafing against the restrictions, a number of news organizations filed suit in January 1991 challenging the legality of the Pentagon press rules. Claiming the rules were in excess of what was necessary to protect national security, the news organizations requested an injunction that would prohibit "hindering any member of the press in coverage of deployment and overt combat by United States forces and prohibiting defendants from excluding the press from areas where United States forces are deployed or engaged in combat"[132] except in instances where security truly would be endangered. The news groups asked the court to strike down the press pool system as unconstitutional. But before federal district court judge Leonard B. Sand could rule, the war ended. Sand therefore dismissed the case, saying that, because the war was not ongoing and the press restrictions were no longer operating, the case was moot.

Despite press complaints about the Pentagon restrictions, some media critics accused the press of having become cheerleaders for the United States during the Persian Gulf War. In fact, even some government officials expressed surprise at the lack of initiative on the part of the news media. Pete Williams, Defense Department spokesman during the conflict, said "the reporting has been largely a recitation of what administration people have said."[133]

"The Real Horror of the Persian Gulf War"

The government claimed, for example, and many journalists reported, that the high-technology weapons used by the United States and allied forces were extremely accurate. Critics note that two major networks, CBS and NBC, declined to broadcast film footage that showed heavy civilian casualties resulting from allied bombing raids. The official government line had been that allied air attacks were highly accurate surgical strikes that minimized civilian deaths. But in June 1997, the General Accounting Office said the Pentagon had overstated the effectiveness of the weapons. Some veteran journalists, however, said press failures during the war were in fact due to government censorship. Walter Cronkite, a highly respected television news anchor for CBS, charged that blatant censorship was "the real horror of the Persian Gulf war."[134]

As the Pentagon Papers case showed in the 1970s and the Gulf War saga demonstrated during the 1990s, the relationship between the press and the government is especially strained during times of war. Legitimate government needs for secrecy to protect the lives of soldiers and military operations collide head-on with the equally legitimate right of the media to report on government decisions that affect the lives of soldiers and their families. The high regard in which the value of free expression is held in the United States was eloquently conveyed by the late Supreme Court Justice Hugo Black:

The U.S. government claimed that the weapons used during the Persian Gulf War were highly accurate and minimized civilian deaths.

Since the earliest days, philosophers have dreamed of a country where the mind and spirit of man would be free; where there would be no limits to inquiry; where men would be free to explore the unknown and to challenge the most deeply rooted beliefs and principles. Our First Amendment was a bold effort to adopt this principle— to establish a country with no legal restrictions of any kind upon the subjects people could investigate, discuss and deny. The Framers knew better perhaps than we do today, the risks they were taking. They knew that free speech might be the friend of change and revolution. But they also knew that it is always the deadliest enemy of tyranny. With this knowledge they still believed that the ultimate happiness and security of a nation lies in its ability to explore, to change, to grow and ceaselessly to adapt itself to new knowledge born of inquiry free from any kind of governmental control over the mind and spirit of man. Loyalty comes from love of good government, not fear of a bad one.[135]

Notes

Intro: "I've decided to Go Ahead"

1. Quoted in David Rudenstine, *The Day the Presses Stopped: A History of the Pentagon Papers Case*. Berkeley: University of California Press, 1996, p. 55.
2. Quoted in Sanford J. Ungar, *The Papers and The Papers: An Account of the Legal and Political Battle over the Pentagon Papers*. New York: E. P. Dutton, 1972, p. 107.
3. Quoted in Ungar, *The Papers and The Papers*, p. 107.

Chapter One: The First Casualty of War

4. Quoted in Geoffrey C. Ward with Ric Burns and Ken Burns, *The Civil War: An Illustrated History*, 6th ed. New York: Alfred A. Knopf, 1990, p. 16.
5. Quoted in William O. Douglas, *An Almanac of Liberty*. Garden City, NY: Doubleday, 1954, p. 63.
6. Quoted in Joseph J. Mathews, *Reporting the Wars*. Minneapolis, University of Minnesota Press, 1957, p. 80.
7. William Tecumseh Sherman, *Sherman: Memoirs of General W. T. Sherman*, 2d ed. New York: Library of America, 1990, p. 899.
8. Sherman, *Sherman*, p. 899.
9. Quoted in Zechariah Chafee Jr., *Free Speech in the United States*, 5th ed. Cambridge, MA: Harvard University Press, 1954, p. 40.
10. Quoted in Elder Witt, ed., *Congressional Quarterly's Guide to the U.S. Supreme Court*. Washington, DC: Congressional Quarterly, 1979, p. 392.
11. Quoted in Harold L. Nelson, ed., *Freedom of the Press from Hamilton to the Warren Court*. Indianapolis: Bobbs-Merrill, 1967, p. 265.
12. Quoted in Bruce Cumings, *War and Television*. London: Verso, 1992, p. 83.
13. Quoted in Stanley Karnow, *Vietnam: A History*. New York: Viking Press, 1983, p. 489.
14. Quoted in Karnow, *Vietnam*, p. 547.

15. William H. Rehnquist, *All the Laws but One: Civil Liberties in Wartime.* New York: Alfred A. Knopf, 1998, p. 218.

16. Quoted in Karnow, *Vietnam,* p. 633.

17. Quoted in Cumings, *War and Television,* p. 84.

Chapter Two: A Threat to National Security

18. Quoted in Rudenstine, *The Day The Presses Stopped,* p. 71.

19. Quoted in Rudenstine, *The Day The Presses Stopped,* p. 72.

20. Quoted in Rudenstine, *The Day The Presses Stopped,* p. 81.

21. Quoted in Ungar, *The Papers and The Papers,* pp. 123–24.

22. Quoted in Ungar, *The Papers and The Papers,* p. 125.

23. Quoted in Ungar, *The Papers and The Papers,* pp. 125–26.

24. Quoted in Ungar, *The Papers and The Papers,* p. 128.

25. Quoted in Rudenstine, *The Day the Presses Stopped,* p. 105.

26. Quoted in Ungar, *The Papers and The Papers,* p. 129.

27. Quoted in Rudenstine, *The Day the Presses Stopped,* p. 106.

28. Quoted in Ungar, *The Papers and The Papers,* p. 129.

29. Quoted in Rudenstine, *The Day the Presses Stopped,* p. 107.

30. Quoted in Ungar, *The Papers and The Papers,* p. 129.

31. Quoted in Rudenstine, *The Day the Presses Stopped,* p. 141.

32. Quoted in Rudenstine, *The Day the Presses Stopped,* p. 143.

33. Quoted in Rudenstine, *The Day the Presses Stopped,* p. 143.

34. Quoted in Rudenstine, *The Day the Presses Stopped,* pp. 143–44.

35. Quoted in Ungar, *The Papers and The Papers,* p. 171.

36. Quoted in Rudenstine, *The Day the Presses Stopped,* p. 158.

37. Quoted in Ungar, *The Papers and The Papers,* p. 174.

38. Quoted in Ungar, *The Papers and The Papers,* p. 175.

39. Quoted in Rodney A. Smolla, *Free Speech in an Open Society.* New York: Alfred A. Knopf, 1992, p. 252.

Chapter Three: Government Warns of Wartime Complications

40. Quoted in Ungar, *The Papers and The Papers,* p. 230.

41. Quoted in Ungar, *The Papers and The Papers,* p. 231.

42. Quoted in Rudenstine, *The Day the Presses Stopped,* p. 270.

43. Quoted in Rudenstine, *The Day the Presses Stopped,* p. 271.

44. Quoted in William J. Small, *Political Power and the Press.* New York: W. W. Norton, 1972, pp. 281–82.

45. Quoted in Small, *Political Power and the Press*, pp. 284–85.
46. Quoted in Ungar, *The Papers and The Papers*, p. 237.
47. Quoted in Ungar, *The Papers and The Papers*, pp. 237–38.
48. Norman Redlich and Bernard Schwartz, eds., *Constitutional Law: Volume II*. New York: Matthew Bender, 1983, pp. 10-211 – 10-212.
49. Quoted in Small, *Political Power and the Press*, p. 283.
50. Quoted in Small, *Political Power and the Press*, p. 282.
51. Quoted in Small, *Political Power and the Press*, p. 276.
52. Quoted in Peter Irons and Stephanie Guitton, eds., *May It Please the Court: The Most Significant Oral Arguments Made Before the Supreme Court Since 1955*. New York: The New Press, 1993, p. 169.
53. Quoted in Irons and Guitton, *May It Please the Court*, p. 169.
54. Quoted in Small, *Political Power and the Press*, p. 276.
55. Quoted in Small, *Political Power and the Press*, p. 277.
56. Quoted in Bob Woodward and Scott Armstrong, *The Brethren: Inside the Supreme Court*. New York: Simon and Schuster, 1979, p. 143.
57. Quoted in Irons and Guitton, *May It Please the Court*, p. 171.
58. Quoted in Bernard Schwartz, *The Ascent of Pragmatism: The Burger Court in Action*, 2d ed. Reading, MA: Addison-Wesley, 1990, p. 160.
59. Quoted in Ungar, *The Papers and The Papers*, p. 243.
60. Quoted in Schwartz, *The Ascent of Pragmatism*, p. 161.
61. Quoted in Schwartz, *The Ascent of Pragmatism*, p. 161.
62. Quoted in Ungar, *The Papers and The Papers*, p. 244.
63. Quoted in Small, *Political Power and the Press*, p. 278.
64. Quoted in Small, *Political Power and the Press*, p. 278.
65. Quoted in Irons and Guitton, *May It Please the Court*, p. 175.
66. Quoted in Irons and Guitton, *May It Please the Court*, p. 175.

Chapter Four: The *Times* Disputes Government Authority

67. Quoted in Ungar, *The Papers and The Papers*, p. 234.
68. Quoted in Rudenstine, *The Day the Presses Stopped*, p. 280.
69. Quoted in Rudenstine, *The Day the Presses Stopped*, p. 281.
70. Quoted in Ungar, *The Papers and The Papers*, pp. 238–39.

71. Quoted in Ungar, *The Papers and The Papers*, p. 239.
72. Quoted in Rudenstine, *The Day the Presses Stopped*, p. 277.
73. Quoted in Ungar, *The Papers and The Papers*, p. 239.
74. Quoted in Rudenstine, *The Day the Presses Stopped*, p. 290.
75. Quoted in Rudenstine, *The Day the Presses Stopped*, p. 290.
76. Quoted in Irons and Guitton, *May It Please the Court*, p. 172.
77. Quoted in Rudenstine, *The Day the Presses Stopped*, p. 291.
78. Quoted in Irons and Guitton, *May It Please the Court*, p. 173.
79. Quoted in Rudenstine, *The Day the Presses Stopped*, p. 292.
80. Quoted in Irons and Guitton, *May It Please the Court*, p. 173.
81. Quoted in Irons and Guitton, *May It Please the Court*, p. 173.
82. Quoted in Irons and Guitton, *May It Please the Court*, p. 173.
83. Quoted in Irons and Guitton, *May It Please the Court*, pp. 173–74.
84. Quoted in Rudenstine, *The Day the Presses Stopped*, p. 294.
85. Quoted in Rudenstine, *The Day the Presses Stopped*, p. 294.
86. Quoted in Rudenstine, *The Day the Presses Stopped*, p. 294.
87. Quoted in Ungar, *The Papers and The Papers*, p. 245.
88. Quoted in Irons and Guitton, *May It Please the Court*, p. 174.
89. Quoted in Rudenstine, *The Day the Presses Stopped*, p. 295.
90. Quoted in Rudenstine, *The Day the Presses Stopped*, p. 295.
91. Quoted in Rudenstine, *The Day the Presses Stopped*, p. 295.
92. Quoted in Rudenstine, *The Day the Presses Stopped*, p. 296.
93. Quoted in Irons and Guitton, *May It Please the Court*, p. 174.
94. Quoted in Ungar, *The Papers and The Papers*, p. 246.
95. Quoted in Irons and Guitton, *May It Please the Court*, p. 175.

Chapter Five: The Supreme Court Speaks as One — and Individually

96. Quoted in Witt, *Congressional Quarterly's Guide to the U.S. Supreme Court*, p. 430.
97. Quoted in Woodward and Armstrong, *The Brethren*, p. 146.
98. William O. Douglas, *The Court Years 1939–1975: The Autobiography of William O. Douglas*. New York: Random House, 1980, p. 207.
99. Quoted in Schwartz, *The Ascent of Pragmatism*, p. 159.

100. Quoted in Rudenstine, *The Day the Presses Stopped*, p. 298.
101. Quoted in Rudenstine, *The Day the Presses Stopped*, p. 299.
102. Quoted in Redlich and Schwartz, *Constitutional Law*, pp. 10-216–10-217.
103. Quoted in Redlich and Schwartz, *Constitutional Law*, p. 10-217.
104. Quoted in Redlich and Schwartz, *Constitutional Law*, p. 10-217.
105. Quoted in Redlich and Schwartz, *Constitutional Law*, p. 10-219.
106. Quoted in Redlich and Schwartz, *Constitutional Law*, p. 10-222.
107. Quoted in Redlich and Schwartz, *Constitutional Law*, p. 10-223.
108. Quoted in Redlich and Schwartz, *Constitutional Law*, p. 10-224.
109. Quoted in Smolla, *Free Speech in an Open Society*, p. 258.
110. Quoted in Redlich and Schwartz, *Constitutional Law*, p. 10-226.
111. Quoted in Redlich and Schwartz, *Constitutional Law*, p. 10-227.
112. Quoted in Redlich and Schwartz, *Constitutional Law*, p. 10-231.
113. Quoted in Redlich and Schwartz, *Constitutional Law*, p. 10-233.
114. Quoted in Redlich and Schwartz, *Constitutional Law*, p. 10-234.
115. Quoted in Redlich and Schwartz, *Constitutional Law*, pp. 10-234–10-235.
116. Quoted in Smolla, *Free Speech in an Open Society*, p. 263.
117. Quoted in Redlich and Schwartz, *Constitutional Law*, p. 10-236.
118. Quoted in Redlich and Schwartz, *Constitutional Law*, p. 10-239.
119. Quoted in Harold L. Nelson and Dwight L. Teeter Jr., *Law of Mass Communications: Freedom and Control of Print and Broadcast Media*, 3d ed. Mineola, NY: The Foundation Press, 1978, p. 48.

Chapter Six: Legacy of the Pentagon Papers Case

120. Quoted in Ungar, *The Papers and The Papers*, p. 260.
121. Quoted in Ungar, *The Papers and The Papers*, p. 262.
122. Quoted in Rudenstine, *The Day the Presses Stopped*, p. 339.
123. Paul McMasters, telephone interview with author, Arlington, VA, August 18, 1999.
124. Quoted in Redlich and Schwartz, *Constitutional Law*, p. 10-245.
125. Quoted in Smolla, *Free Speech in an Open Society*, p. 265.
126. Quoted in Smolla, *Free Speech in an Open Society*, p. 267.
127. Quoted in Smolla, *Free Speech in an Open Society*, p. 267.
128. Quoted in Smolla, *Free Speech in an Open Society*, p. 268.

129. Quoted in Eve Pell, *The Big Chill*. Boston: Beacon Press, 1984, p. 65.

130. Quoted in Smolla, *Free Speech in an Open Society*, p. 314.

131. Quoted in Smolla, *Free Speech in an Open Society*, p. 292.

132. Quoted in Smolla, *Free Speech in an Open Society*, p. 297.

133. Quoted in Carl Jensen, *20 Years of Censored News*. New York: Seven Stories Press, 1997, p. 248.

134. Quoted in Jensen, *20 Years of Censored News*, p. 264.

135. Quoted in Small, *Political Power and the Press*, p. 402.

Timeline

1967
Defense Secretary McNamara orders study of U.S. involvement in Vietnam.

1968
McNamara leaves Defense Department.

1969
Pentagon Papers study completed. Daniel Ellsberg photocopies study.

1971
March: Ellsberg gives copy of study to *Times*.

June 13: Times first publishes stories based on study.

June 15: Times enjoined from further publication.

June 18: Post publishes its first stories based on study, then is enjoined.

June 19: Judge Gurfein rules for *Times*; appeals court extends injunction.

June 21: Judge Gesell rules for *Post*; appeals court extends injunction.

June 23: Appeals court sends *Times* case back to Gurfein; appeals court in *Post* case rules for paper but extends stay.

June 24: Times appeals ruling in its case to Supreme Court; government appeals to Supreme Court in *Post* case.

June 25: Supreme Court agrees to decide the two cases.

June 26: Supreme Court hears arguments in the two cases.

June 28: Ellsberg indicted for violations of Espionage Act.

June 29: Senator Gravel releases portions of Pentagon Papers to media.

June 30: Supreme Court rules for *Times* and *Post*.

1973
May 11: Case against Ellsberg dismissed because of government misconduct.

For Further Reading

Books

Leah Farish, *The First Amendment: Freedom of Speech, Religion, and the Press.* Springfield, NJ: Enslow, 1998. Examines the many facets of, and challenges to, the First Amendment and includes a short discussion of the Pentagon Papers case.

David F. Forte, *The Supreme Court.* New York: Franklin Watts, 1979. Examines the Supreme Court, its role in American history, and its influence on American life, with a short narrative on the Pentagon Papers case.

D. J. Herda, *New York Times v. United States: National Security and Censorship.* Hillside, NJ: Enslow, 1994. Examines the tensions between freedom of the press and national security via the Pentagon Papers case.

Olga G. and Edwin P. Hoyt, *Freedom of the News Media.* New York: Seabury Press, 1973. Broad overview of tensions between the press and government, including a chapter on the Pentagon Papers case.

Philip A. Klinker, *The American Heritage History of the Bill of Rights: The First Amendment.* Englewood Cliffs, NJ: Silver Burdett Press, 1991. Comprehensive overview of the Bill of Rights and the First Amendment in particular, including a look at the Pentagon Papers case.

Jethro K. Lieberman, *Free Speech, Free Press, and the Law.* New York: Lothrup, Lee and Shepard Books, 1980. Examines fifty cases that demonstrate how the Supreme Court has interpreted free press and free speech guarantees, including a short examination of the Pentagon Papers case.

Edmund Lindop, *The Bill of Rights and Landmark Cases.* New York: Franklin Watts, 1989. An overview of constitutional guarantees of liberty and the Supreme Court's interpretation of those rights, with a short look at the Pentagon Papers case.

Websites

University of Oregon (http://ballmer.uoregon.edu/tgleason/j385/pentagon.htm). Includes copy of the per curiam opinion in the

Pentagon Papers case plus links to the individual opinions of each justice in the case.

First Amendment Center (www.freedomforum.org). A website devoted to covering legal issues relating to the constitutionally guaranteed right to free speech and free press.

Works Consulted

Books

Liva Baker, *The Justice from Beacon Hill: The Life and Times of Oliver Wendell Holmes*. New York: HarperCollins, 1991. An intriguing examination of one of the nation's preeminent jurists.

Randy E. Barnett, ed., *The Rights Retained by the People: The History and Meaning of the Ninth Amendment*. Fairfax, VA: George Mason University Press, 1989. Provocative writings by authors from James Madison to constitutional scholar Norman Redlich on the meaning of the Ninth Amendment.

Irving Brant, *The Bill of Rights: Its Origin and Meaning*. Indianapolis: Bobbs-Merrill, 1965. A thorough examination of the guarantees of liberty contained in the Constitution's first ten amendments.

Lincoln Caplan, *The Tenth Justice: The Solicitor General and the Rule of Law*. New York: Alfred A. Knopf, 1987. An intriguing look at the office of the solicitor general and those who have held the office.

Zechariah Chafee Jr., *Free Speech in the United States*, 5th ed. Cambridge, MA: Harvard University Press, 1954. A First Amendment scholar examines the stresses on the First Amendment during times of perceived national crisis.

Bruce Cumings, *War and Television*. London: Verso, 1992. A look at how television has helped change attitudes about war.

William B. Dickinson Jr., ed., *Watergate: Chronology of a Crisis*. Washington, DC: Congressional Quarterly, 1973. Comprehensive examination of the Watergate scandal.

William O. Douglas, *A Living Bill of Rights*. Garden City, NY: Doubleday, 1961. One of the nation's foremost libertarians offers commentary on the ongoing quest for freedom in the United States.

William O. Douglas, *An Almanac of Liberty*. Garden City, NY: Doubleday, 1954. A compendium of daily meditations celebrating freedoms by the late Supreme Court justice.

William O. Douglas, *The Court Years 1939–1975: The Autobiography of William O. Douglas*. New York: Random House, 1980.

The late Supreme Court justice, a champion of individual liberty during thirty-six years on the Court, provides his insights on the Court's work.

Thomas M. Franck and Edward Weisband, eds., *Secrecy and Foreign Policy*. London: Oxford University Press, 1974. A variety of experts examine ways to balance the government's right to govern and the people's right to know.

Morton H. Halperin and Daniel N. Hoffman, *Top Secret: National Security and the Right to Know*. Washington, DC: New Republic Books, 1977. Sweeping critique of government secrecy abuses and suggestions for fixing the system.

Alexander Hamilton, James Madison, and John Jay, *The Federalist Papers*. Edited by Benjamin Fletcher Wright. Cambridge, MA: Belknap Press, 1961. A collection of essays written from 1787 and 1788 offering arguments in favor of the adoption of the Constitution by the states.

Edward G. Hudon, *Freedom of Speech and Press in America*. Washington, DC: Public Affairs Press, 1963. A good overview of the inherent tensions between the government's need to preserve order and the rights of citizens to speak out and to be informed by the press.

Peter Irons and Stephanie Guitton, eds., *May It Please the Court: The Most Significant Oral Arguments Made Before the Supreme Court Since 1955*. New York: The New Press, 1993. Provides transcripts, accompanied by cassette tapes, of oral arguments in twenty-three landmark Supreme Court cases.

Leon Jaworski, *The Right and the Power: The Prosecution of Watergate*. New York: Reader's Digest, 1976. Special Prosecutor Leon Jaworski provides an insider's glimpse into the crimes of the Nixon White House that led to the resignation of the president.

Thomas Jefferson, *Thomas Jefferson: In His Own Words*. Edited by Maureen Harrison and Steve Gilbert. New York: Barnes and Noble, 1993. A wide range of writings from one of the nation's founders.

Carl Jenson, *20 Years of Censored News*. New York: Seven Stories Press, 1997. A critique of the performance of the American press from 1976 to 1996.

Stanley Karnow, *Vietnam: A History*. New York: Viking Press, 1983. A comprehensive look at the Vietnamese civil war.

Joseph J. Mathews, *Reporting the Wars*. Minneapolis: University of Minnesota Press, 1957. A look at the hazards, restrictions, and difficulties of war reporting.

John Stuart Mill, *On Liberty*. Edited by David Spitz. New York: W. W. Norton, 1975. This influential essay argues that freedom of speech is essential to discover truth.

Harold L. Nelson, ed., *Freedom of the Press from Hamilton to the Warren Court*. Indianapolis: Bobbs-Merrill, 1967. A look at ongoing tensions between the press and government throughout U.S. history.

Harold L. Nelson and Dwight L. Teeter Jr., *Law of Mass Communications: Freedom and Control of Print and Broadcast Media*, 3d ed. Mineola, NY: The Foundation Press, 1978. A good overview of the law governing free speech rights.

Eve Pell, *The Big Chill*. Boston: Beacon Press, 1984. Intriguing analysis of the confluence of forces at work to undermine First Amendment freedoms.

Norman Redlich and Bernard Schwartz, eds., *Constitutional Law: Volume II*. New York: Matthew Bender, 1983. Noted constitutional scholars present commentaries and edited opinions of the United States Supreme Court.

William H. Rehnquist, *All the Laws but One: Civil Liberties in Wartime*. New York: Alfred A. Knopf, 1998. Supreme Court justice Rehnquist examines how wartime stresses have threatened civil liberties in America.

David Rudenstine, *The Day the Presses Stopped: A History of the Pentagon Papers Case*. Berkeley: University of California Press, 1996. Comprehensive analysis of one of the most dramatic confrontations between the press and government in American history.

Peter Schrag, *Test of Loyalty: Daniel Ellsberg and the Rituals of Secret Government*. New York: Simon and Schuster, 1974. Provides a sweeping look at the criminal trial of Daniel Ellsberg.

Bernard Schwartz, *The Ascent of Pragmatism: The Burger Court in Action*, 2d ed. Reading, MA: Addison-Wesley, 1990. A noted scholar examines the decisions of the Supreme Court under Chief Justice Warren Burger.

William Tecumseh Sherman, *Sherman: Memoirs of General W. T. Sherman*, 2d ed. New York: Library of America, 1990. Comprehensive and vivid accounts of controversial Civil War general's life and wartime experiences.

William J. Small, *Political Power and the Press*. New York: W. W. Norton, 1972. Examines tensions between the press and government.

Rodney A. Smolla, *Free Speech in an Open Society*. New York: Alfred A. Knopf, 1992. A constitutional scholar provides a broad overview of challenges to free speech in an increasingly globalized and technology-driven world.

Sanford J. Ungar, *The Papers and The Papers: An Account of the Legal and Political Battle over the Pentagon Papers*. New York: E. P. Dutton, 1972. Comprehensive look at the personalities and events behind the celebrated Pentagon Papers case.

Geoffrey C. Ward with Ric Burns and Ken Burns, *The Civil War: An Illustrated History*, 6th ed. New York: Alfred A. Knopf, 1990. Broad and poignant overview of the nation's violent war between the states.

Juan Williams, *Thurgood Marshall: American Revolutionary*. New York: Times Books, 1998. A thorough and vivid account of the life of a civil rights leader.

Elder Witt, ed., *Congressional Quarterly's Guide to the U.S. Supreme Court*. Washington, DC: Congressional Quarterly, 1979. A broad examination of the Supreme Court, its major opinions and the justices who have served on it.

Bob Woodward and Scott Armstrong, *The Brethren: Inside the Supreme Court*. New York: Simon and Schuster, 1979. The first detailed look at the inner workings of one of the nation's most secret government institutions.

Periodicals

First Amendment Center, *State of the First Amendment, 1999*.

Internet Sources

Freedom Forum, "Judge Lifts Order Barring Newspaper from Publishing Story," by The Associated Press, August 17, 1999. www.freedomforum.org/press/1999/8/17castoryban.asp.

Public Broadcasting System, *Frontline*, "James Goodale, General Counsel for the *New York Times* During the Pentagon Papers Case," 1999. www.pbs.org/wgbh/pages/frontline/smoke/interviews/goodale1.html.

University of California–Berkeley Institute of International Studies, "Reflections on the Vietnam War: Presidential Decisions and Public Dissent—Conversations with Daniel Ellsberg," 1998. http:globetrotter.berkeley.edu/people/Ellsberg/ellsberg98-0. html.

FindLaw, "U.S. Supreme Court: *Texas v. Johnson*, 491 U.S. 397 (1989)." http://laws.findlaw.com/US/491/397.html.

Websites

Hedrick Smith Productions (www.hedricksmith.com).

First Amendment Project (www.thefirstamendment.org).

Indiana University-Purdue University, Walter E. Helmke Library (www.lib.ipfw.indiana.edu/pirs/fed/1stamwww.html).

Index

uthor

riter whose work most
r-Telegram, where he is a
regularly published in
nal, the magazine of the
Ir. Campbell worked in
Bond Buyer, where he
ith his wife, Linda, and
e, in Fort Worth, Texas,
ing youth sports.

About the A

Geoffrey A. Campbell is a freelance commonly appears in the *Fort Worth S* senior book reviewer. He also has be the *World Book Yearbook* and in *ABA Jo* American Bar Association. Previously, Washington, D.C., as a reporter for t covered the Supreme Court. He lives the couple's twins, Kirby and Macken where he is active in the PTA and coa